ID0768007

PATHFINDER

*A Guide to a Successful Career
for First-Generation Immigrants*

LUCY CHEN

Pathfinder: A Guide to a Successful Career for First-Generation Immigrants
Lucy Chen

Lucy Chen was selected by the National Diversity Council in 2021 as among the "Top 50 Most Powerful Women in Technology."

The stories of five first-generation pioneers illustrate the challenges faced by new immigrants eager to succeed in American business. They are pathfinders embarking on journeys that are filled with demographic, social, and economical challenges. They show managers moving up to manage managers and learning to deal with senior management challenges. The stories honestly reveal the norms, communication styles, mindsets, and politics of corporate business to help other brave souls newly embarking on the same path. These are not things taught in business schools; they are the life experiences of a generation.

www.myPathfinder.net

Print ISBN: 978-1-66786-721-2
eBook ISBN: 978-1-66786-722-9

Printed in the United States of America on SFI Certified paper.
Second Edition

CONTENTS

ACKNOWLEDGEMENTS

I would like to thank my many friends and professional colleagues that I have had the pleasure of getting to know while on my journeys. My conversations with these remarkable individuals were the inspirations for this book.

I am so grateful to my students at the Viswise Academy for their willingness to learn and apply the ideas and concepts I offered to them. These pioneers and leaders dedicate their hard work to cultivate a learning environment for first-generation immigrants in the United States living and working in American business corporations. They immerse themselves and their families in a non-native environment while learning in American education institutions and striving to advance in a new world.

Eternal thanks also go to Ryan, Amy, and Yanan for their contributions and extraordinary support. They helped me develop the core of this book, and their valuable suggestions helped me polish the stories. Amy has been a strong advocate of my stories and a key editor and contributor. Ryan inspired me and refined the stories from the perspective of second-generation Americans, so that they resonate with the new generation.

Many thanks to Angelina Huang, the founder of Viswise Academy, for creating a wonderful learning community. Finally, thanks to Caroline Benton and Barbara Little Liu, my lovely friends, who supported me in bringing this story to life.

INTRODUCTION

Most first-generation Americans harbor lofty ambitions when they begin their journey to America. These individuals have impeccable academic and professional careers because they have aced rigorous exams. Their outstanding performance has placed them at the top of their class in universities, and their college years have earned them high honors from their classmates, professors, and families. Without a doubt, expectations are high for these proud individuals.

The honor of coming to America is not easily earned, and these young trailblazers feel pressure to succeed and prove that the sacrifice of their parents and past generations has not been in vain. As the cream of the crop, professional achievement is not just expected for these young people, it is considered a duty.

Ambiguity and obstacles await them as they embark on their professional journey in America. What are the challenges for these young, ambitious, first-generation immigrant pioneers, and how can they overcome the barriers of learning, language, and culture? How can they compete in a fierce work environment, earn recognition, and advance to senior management in corporate America?

Many new era immigrants are firmly ensconced in the tech headquarters of the world known as Silicon Valley. Many find themselves in fintech in New York. The simple act of speaking can make many first-generation immigrants feel the divide between them and their colleagues. However, they find their careers hindered and distant from their high expectations because of the challenges they face climbing the American corporate ladder. This is largely because American culture is totally different from the first-generation immigrants' homeland, particularly where business is concerned. Their upbringing in Asia and the Middle East does not support the American corporate culture of showmanship, and this is the fundamental cultural difference that causes first-generation immigrants in high tech and financial companies to experience hidden yet mounting challenges in the western corporate environment.

Many Chinese, Japanese, Korean and other Asians consider returning to their homeland where they can advance naturally without the glass ceiling, but as their careers progress, and their second-generation American born children mature, conflicts over where to live and raise their children threaten family unity. The first-generation Americans chase their dreams and become business leaders who are attracted to the career advancement that a return to their home countries would bring, but their second-generation children identify more with American culture than the land of their forefathers. These and other challenges for first-generation families are discussed in this book.

Among these first-generation immigrants are Chinese students who began to arrive in the United States after 1972 during Gerald R. Ford's presidency when China opened the door for young Chinese individuals to study in America. In the 1980s, more Chinese scholars journeyed to America and other overseas countries for academic and scientific research work. For America, Chinese students were a new business and academic market. The 1990s saw an influx of Chinese students in America with increasing influence.

They were trailblazers. They were brave, intelligent, and curious, and their experiences represent fascinating case studies for later generations. Today's Asian-Americans who are entering and navigating western business can learn and build upon the experiences of those who came before them.

It is easy to dream of a successful career, but it is difficult to turn the dream into a reality. There are many steps involved in transforming a dream into an accomplished career, and it takes relentless persistence. These first-generation immigrants have to be stubborn and wise. They must refuse to compromise on their dream yet be flexible enough to achieve it. A flexible approach is crucial because some of their early ideas and assumptions about what they thought they wanted might have been wrong. They will have to adapt to unexpected situations. It will require a lot of hard work. There is no cookie-cutter approach, and they all need to pave their own way to success.

This book contains the stories of five first-generation immigrant pioneers. I use their experiences to show the challenges in transitioning to a different culture and environment. I show how managers move up to manage managers. I describe their journeys and a relocation experience to Beijing. I also show how these pioneers deal with senior management challenges. My goal is to share and convey what I have learned to other brave souls navigating a similar path. This book is an honest conversation that reveals the norms, communication styles, mindsets, and politics of the corporate business universe. These are not things taught in business schools; they are the life experiences of a generation.

This book is based on a fast-paced and competitive environment. It is oriented toward first-generation high tech and business leaders who are working in the ever-changing business world of corporate America. All industries are facing the challenge of machine learning-based digital transformation, and many businesses are evolving into tech companies. Technical first-generation talent, like the individuals described in this book, are the major force for this digital transformation. The cases described here are based on true stories, although the individual names and companies have been changed for reasons of privacy. The facts and experiences are pertinent to all immigrant technical leaders in the middle of a career, and I hope readers will find a strong connection to where they are now in their own journeys and how to reach their dreams.

PART I.

PREPARING
YOUR CAREER LAUNCH PAD

MICHELLE'S STORY

"You did a great job this year. You might consider improving your English communication skills."

Michelle remembered this comment by her manager from her annual performance review.

Michelle originated from Sichuan Province where she trained and worked as an English teacher. After passing the TOEFL and GRE tests, she obtained a visa to attend Stevens Institute of Technology in New Jersey. A university where she could admire the view of the New York City skyline from her classroom was the start of her American life. While her English language abilities had gotten her this far, Michelle was undergoing a mindset shift to transition from her original teaching career. She had trained to be a teacher like her father, but her new life in America as a non-native speaker had made K-12 teaching less of a viable option. Michelle decided on a career in technology and began studying Management Information Systems (MIS). While attending university, she lived with an American family and spent her days studying full-time and her evenings working part-time, while also helping the family in exchange for tuition support.

Michelle landed an internship at an insurance agency as an international student where she received practical training before graduation. With her new-found knowledge of computers, she created a back-office database system for the agency. After her graduation, Michelle was hired by a tech company as a software engineer. She worked diligently and often 996 (9 am to 9 pm, six days a week) as she learned and absorbed information like a sponge. As an individual contributor, she witnessed reorganizations, mergers, and personnel changes that affected managers, teams, and individual employees. Her environment was constantly evolving. Michelle observed what was going on around her and paved her own career path, looking for challenges and possibilities to move up. However, English business language and American cultural differences often hindered her day-to-day performance.

Overcoming the difficulties, Michelle worked hard and hoped that her efforts would be recognized. She was the "qualified quiet." She obediently did whatever her supervisors required, even to the extent of taking on initiatives that were not asked of her as she went beyond her duties. Michelle had a deep inner drive to become independent and financially successful. She dreamed of how proud her family back home would be when a revered schoolteacher from Sichuan Province conquered western norms and rose through the ranks of corporate America.

1. Envisioning a Future Self

I am convinced that about half of what separates successful entrepreneurs from the non-successful ones is pure perseverance.

---Steve Jobs

———————

Where will Michelle's career take her in five years? As a relatively new or recent entrant into this hectic global workforce, how frequently should Michelle expect to change her job or responsibilities? What should her career path look like? How will her career success affect her personal and professional life?

Michelle was in an intense learning mode as she entered the software industry, but her drive and ultimate goals led her to find the path forward. The typical software engineer finds their responsibilities changing often, sometimes every two weeks in the Agile sprint development model. Michelle witnessed habitual upheaval in the form of reorganizations and leadership changes, which is status quo in the digital age and tech economy. The rate of change was startling for Michelle, who was used to the much more predictable world of teaching back in China. In her now tech role, even when Michelle remained in the same position, she was constantly tasked with new things. She adapted to new technology quickly and was relentlessly consistent. She was reliable and trustworthy despite the constant shifts. Her tasks switched from engineering to operations and back to engineering almost every eighteen months.

As time went on, Michelle thought about making a career change. She considered different types of organizations. Startups were appealing because they promised excitement and opportunity, but would she thrive in a less-structured, fast-paced organization? How could she evaluate whether that was the right work culture for her? What factors should she consider, and what questions should she ask herself?

Growing up in China, Michelle's parents had worked for stable state-owned factories. A private startup was not a risk she thought she could take. Michelle thought of ways to navigate her professional growth and plan for her next move. As Michelle learnt how to make the right decisions for her career, she paved the way to success in corporate America.

From time to time, it was not clear how she should best move ahead, but she was persistent in being successful despite difficulty or delay in achieving success. She persevered. She genuinely thought that after the nineteenth try, the twentieth would meet with success.

2. Language and Culture Learning

Michelle was confident that as she progressed in her new career, her vision would become more attainable. First, however, Michelle needed to understand where she was in her personal growth. Michelle's life was still fluid, and her career plan was changing. Transforming from teaching to technology, Michelle learned, readapted, and pivoted as her experiences began to take her in different directions.

One of Michelle's first jobs while she was still attending the Stevens Institute in New Jersey was as an assistant librarian for the Institute. She worked at one of the library's popular reserve desks on campus. There, she learned how to fulfill research requests from professors, and she went the extra mile to learn the background of their projects. She would suggest additional materials as she located requested content in the library. Very soon, Michelle mobilized her hours in the library, and her teaching background trained her to help people with extra effort. She became the favorite go-to person on the library reserve desk for the research professors. She made many friends among the professors who needed library support on research projects. Ultimately, her hard work was rewarded by one of the professors who hired her as a research assistant.

Later, Michelle sought employment outside the college where she could learn more in the business world. Michelle interviewed with a couple who managed a privately owned maintenance shipyard on the Hudson River. The couple needed someone to run the office front desk, track parts, schedule the delivery of goods, and provide some finance support. The interview went well, and the couple were profoundly impressed with Michelle's attention to details and her current studies in computer networks. They were keen to use her computer skills, digitize the financial paper flow process, and to convert some of the Excel and Word customers online. Michelle seemed like the perfect person for the job, and the couple began to prepare the paperwork for an offer. As the three of them were discussing the terms of employment, the husband asked Michelle,

"By the way, have you done bookkeeping?"

"Yes!" said Michelle, excited that she could be of even more value to the couple. "I love books. I worked in a library and knew exactly how the library back-end systems physically arrange the books so that they are ordered and easy to find."

The couple looked at each other and then at Michelle. Their faces showed a mix of alarm and sympathy as they realized the huge communication hurdle in front of them. This miscommunication showed that Michelle would face significant obstacles understanding what was being asked of her, and they feared that a dangerous shipyard where the vertical knowledge learning curve would be steep was not the right training ground for her. They told Michelle that they would think about her application and be in touch. Michelle never heard from them again.

———————

First-generation immigrants working in America are at a disadvantage when it comes to communication in the workplace, as English is their second language. Finding the right vocabulary during spontaneous real-time debate and meeting interactions is difficult. Some Asians, especially females, hesitate to speak up, as English is not their native language, and this causes misunderstandings, bottlenecks, and even costly missed opportunities. The spoken words alone can make many first-generation immigrants feel the divide between themselves and their co-workers. When adding culturally specific behaviors and styles of responding to questions, colleagues assume that they don't share the same level of understanding of projects as other team members, which may lead to the feeling of being left out.

When conversing, many new language learners first convert English into their native language before speaking. That translation process takes time. In order to communicate freely with no time delay, new language learners have to overcome this instinct and learn to think and reason in English. It takes a few years to actively train the mind to instantly convert without translating back and forth between their native language and English.

Moreover, the consequence of trying to find the precise words to explain an idea is that much of the rich thinking behind the concept is lost. For example, the meaning of "agile" in English is quite different to its meaning in Chinese in direct translation. When filtering it into Chinese, agile means fast or quick with one meaning, which removes much of the real nuances of the term in English.

Michelle was an experienced teacher with an advanced education and established skills. She pursued further education and brand-new skills in a new industry. Despite this, her previous expertise was insufficient in her new western environment. Michelle realized her lack of fluent language communication skills. She knew that she was going to need a lot longer to master the language and understand western culture with all its peculiarities. Her intelligent mind was blurred by her language communication difficulties. This was a setback for Michelle as a first-generation immigrant.

Like a professional table tennis player who decides to switch sports and try tennis, Michelle was no longer at the top of her game. Tennis exercises a different group of muscles than table tennis, and even the best tennis player must relearn a whole new game. She may have been a high-flier in China as a teacher, but corporate America required different language skills, different muscle memory, and a more direct communication strategy. She was saddened and disappointed at the prospect of going back to basics and learning anew. She would need to take micro-steps everyday for many years to come to reach her goal. The English language was like a brand new sport for which she needed to retrain her muscles, but she had the experience and maturity to respond. That mindset is critical to identifying what matters most in terms of assimilating and learning in a new country.

3. The "Qualified Quiet"

The stereotypical Asian American is the ultimate worker bee who produces fantastic results. A hard worker like Michelle takes on tasks across functional teams to help avoid catastrophes. She becomes a key problem-solver, a go-to person for all the computer system bugs, yet there is no guarantee that her diligent work will buy her a promotion. Some quiet employees work fifteen years and experience no career advancement. Worker bees are quiet and often passed over for promotion.

Chinese Americans are known as "the qualified quiet." They do their work efficiently, without fuss, and, consequently, without visibility. They are afraid of shining the spotlight on their achievements or voicing their opinions. They wait for things to come, and they wait to be noticed. Meanwhile, deep in their hearts, they long to be promoted.

————

Michelle worked as a software engineer. She was the epitome of the "qualified quiet" and soon advanced to senior software engineer. As her confidence grew, Michelle began to ask her supervisor for additional responsibilities. She found ways to expand her collaboration across peer groups. She coordinated with cross-functional teams and moved horizontally within the organization.

In the dark sea, a lighthouse blinks persistently and strikingly to attract the attention of nearby ships. Michelle learned that if she wanted to be noticed, she had to be visible. She needed to blink like a lighthouse and stand out to attract the attention of management. Michelle did her work so well that her boss had no idea of the scope of her work because everything was so well-managed. She was reliable; meanwhile, she was looking for the opportunity to shine.

The Chinese have a saying: "Gold shines regardless." The saying implies that even if a jewel is buried deep down in the earth, it will eventually be noticed. In fast-paced corporate America, this is viewed as a passive attitude. If Michelle waited to be promoted, she might wait a long time. To advance, in certain situations, she needed to reject the traditional Chinese "Gold shines regardless" mindset and embrace the lighthouse blinking show off mindset.

During her annual review, Michelle noted the desire to advance. Her manager saw her goals and endorsed her idea in the official review. During her annual review conversation with her manager, she also propagated an ongoing conversation and set an objective to review possibilities for advancement every three months. Michelle spoke up and paved the way for additional responsibilities. She manifested her work and stepped out of her comfort zone as a qualified quiet worker to compensate for her language skill. She was prepared to seize any opportunity that would advance her career.

4. Seizing the Moment

Opportunities come in many forms—spearheading a new initiative, moving to a different location, or taking on a mentoring role. Any of these examples could showcase Michelle's ability to take on a new responsibility. During the years of organizational change, Michelle watched her peers move up to manager positions. She kept her eyes open for opportunities and grabbed them to jumpstart her management mindset.

———————

Michelle asked her boss if she could mentor another employee and teach them her role in case, she ever needed backup. She requested that a contractor be hired to take on her responsibilities while she went to Sichuan for a long-awaited home visit. These requests showed foresight and initiative, but they also emphasized the importance of her work and the need to train others to back her up. Michelle's value, and her efforts to mentor and advance others, automatically branded her as a leader. She was prepared to move up as a manager.

———————

The move from an individual contributor to a supervisor is an important leap but also a difficult challenge for anyone. By volunteering to lead an initiative, when a manager position arose, Michelle was prepared, and she applied for the role. Michelle kept an eye out for opportunities outside of her company on LinkedIn, in the next department, at different locations, and overseas. Going from headquarters to a remote office is a particularly valuable opportunity for individual contributor employees because such a move will likely require assuming management of a remote team. When a remote assignment ends, the accompanying experiences and achievements spur advancement.

In America's big tech firms, teams are constantly reshuffled, sometimes every month, and this reshuffling creates new leaders and managers. Michelle was proactive, seized opportunities, and took on new projects. In doing so, she gathered knowledge, confidence, and experience. When a manager position arose, Michelle was the obvious choice among a short list of candidates.

5. Breaking through the Comfort Zone

Michelle learned to be bold and direct, to promote herself and her work, and to be resourceful. She had overcome her shyness and seized opportunities. She did not rely on the linear growth that her Chinese background inferred. Being vocal was necessary so that her product development acumen was not overlooked. She voiced her desire for promotion to technical management and used her achievements as proof of her worth.

Michelle took regular business communication training to improve her communication skills. She took personal training for presentation skills. She watched other co-workers and learned how to present ideas, sprint demos, and retrospectives in meetings so that she was always the voice of her own projects.

At one point, Michelle collaborated on a project with another engineering architect. The architect was from Russia, and English was also his second language just like herself. In the demo, the architect felt that he could not communicate the concept concisely, so he asked Michelle, who had been practicing presentation skills, to explain the concept while the colleague operated the computer.

Because Michelle did the talking, much of the demo and packaging of the product was thoroughly explained by her. She led the demo and supported the architect. Michelle realized that, in this case, the architect needed support in speaking up so that his contribution was recognized. Together with her colleague, Michelle exercised her mentoring and leadership muscles, and she coached the architect in presenting. Because of Michelle's efforts, her team grew to a new level of collaboration and productivity. Michelle, like a lot of first-generation immigrants and minorities, had often been unable to ask her family or networks for relevant professional insights. Therefore, Michelle learned how to find the path of her career on her own.

6. The Right Extra Mile

Drive and perseverance are what separates the wheat from the chaff, but too much drive can eventually backfire. Many first-generation Americans are educated in a way that encourages going the extra mile to work harder than others, but they also must choose the *right* extra mile and do what matters the most. Making that extra phone call, sending that extra email, doing the additional research, helping a customer to upload or download a file, arriving early and staying late; these things are the extra mile, and they require extra time, effort, and a certain mindset.

When Michelle felt exhausted and burned out, she refocused her energies in the right areas. She became more selective as to when she would go the right extra mile. In short, she did "just enough, just in time." Doing just enough, just in time made a huge difference to Michelle, and she became incredibly successful.

———

Michelle was ahead of the game, and she planned how she could attain the knowledge she needed. Michelle was technically strong, she worked with cross-functional teams, such as customer service, operations, finance, marketing, and sales. She exposed herself and learned these functions so that she could improve her cross-functional awareness.

The concept of **T-shaped skills**, or **T-shaped persons,** is a metaphor used to describe the abilities of persons in the workforce. The vertical bar on the letter T represents the depth of related skills and expertise in a single field, whereas the horizontal bar is the ability to collaborate across disciplines with experts in other areas and to apply knowledge in areas of expertise other than one's own.

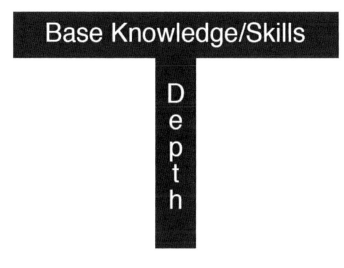

Figure 1. T-Shaped Person Source:
The T-Shaped Person: Building Deep Expertise AND a Wide Knowledge Base By Ransom Patterson

Michelle's T-shape is composed of her technical skills, which form the vertical part of the T, and her cross-functional skills, which form the horizontal part of the T. Michelle does not need to be an expert in every horizontal part of the T as well as the vertical, she needs only a working knowledge of those areas.

Michelle knew that she couldn't be the best at everything, but she chose the right expert area where she *could* be the best in the company. This is a strategic process, and some knowledge takes a long time to master. Choosing the right things to do and letting go of the wrong things was critical to her success in getting to where she wanted to be.

Summary

Michelle was a first-generation immigrant from China. She came to the United States as a student and began her career hoping to live the American dream. She found herself in an unfamiliar cultural environment. Michelle overcame huge cultural barriers as she entered the American workforce.

After graduating from college, those entering the American corporate job market face career unknowns. There are cases of "an ace in the hole," but many first-generation immigrant workers won't have that experience. Michelle prepared her career launch pad by seizing opportunities. She learned the implications of being the qualified quiet as opposed to being visible. She learned to blink like a lighthouse so that she was noticed. She stepped out of her comfort zone and honed her language and communication skills diligently. Most of all, her hardwork and perseverance helped her and many first-generation immigrants to achieve their goals. She went the extra mile, but made sure it was the right mile. What Michelle did was adjust her mindset early in her career. As the organization changed and teams became more agile and mobile, she identified her priorities and did what mattered the most.

PART II.

THE APPEAL OF STARTUPS

MARK'S STORY

Mark was not specifically looking to move into a startup company when an old friend introduced him to Leo, the CEO and cofounder of SuperTech, a venture-backed startup that specializes in augmented reality for education.

Mark was content and proud as a senior engineer within a larger social media company. He had little interest in meeting Leo initially, but he did so out of respect for his friend. Mark ultimately met with Leo several times because he thought it wise to check out virtual reality (VR) and learn about the technology even though his current job was not directly related to the world of VR.

Mark found the initial conversations interesting, so he did more research. He tried the augmented reality hardware set and the subscription games just like a customer would. He thought that if the company and its products were a hit and had the potential to gain rapid market share, he would know after trying them firsthand.

Mark was also curious about the company's culture and organization. Who worked at the startup other than Leo? Mark got to know some of the team members at social events and some competitor webinars that he attended. These experiences helped him better understand the market, the management structure, and how the company functioned.

Mark knew his current job well; he could envision where he would be in five years. Now, he also had a sense of how he would feel if he moved to the energetic and potentially more impactful role at a new company. He considered the changes in compensation and lifestyle at the startup. He tried to gauge the standard of living he could expect considering a mortgage, the cost of his children's education, and the potential benefits he would receive if the startup was successful and went public.

When Leo was ready to make an offer, Mark had already changed his original assumptions about Leo and the startup. During the conversations, he made sure that he was not only a fit for the company, but the company would have the right person for the job. He thought about his previous experience with products, projects, and companies, and he felt that he would thrive in a startup while others might not. Because it was risky, Mark had to do his homework in making sure he was the right man for the job. With his wife's support, he took on the challenge of the architect role and later became a director of SuperTech's flagship product.

Mark's bet for the startup paid off in a few years. He earned the title he wanted and was well respected by his CEO and the executive team. He went to work every day confident that he was making decisions that mattered. He could see his footprint in the company's product.

7. The Perfect Fit

As a computer science graduate from Carnegie Mellon University in Silicon Valley, joining a startup early in his career was not Mark's first choice. A few years later, as he considered a career change, Mark was looking at different types of organizations. Startups were appealing because of the excitement and opportunity they offered, but would he thrive in a less-structured, fast-paced organization? How could he evaluate whether that was the right environment for him? What factors should he consider? What were the right questions to ask himself?

There was a time when taking a job at a startup was viewed as risky, even foolish. Many Chinese people who grew up during the Cultural Revolution experienced lifelong employment in state-owned factories and businesses. Silicon Valley, on the other hand, had produced the biggest companies in the world in the age of digital transformation, and the wave of startups was exploding. Joining a pre-IPO startup that goes public is equivalent to striking gold. Not all startups reach an IPO, and Mark could have lost everything. When he was enthusiastic about the opportunity, everyone inside the company was with him in wanting the company to do well. He needed to weigh the excitement, the timing, the market conditions, and the leadership credibility of the startup.

Mark asked himself the following questions before taking the jump:

1. *"What is my motivation for joining a startup?"*

2. *"Is this role a good fit at this stage in my life?"*

3. *"Do I like the people, the startup culture, and the 996 schedule?"*

4. *"Not all startups make it to an IPO. What are the financial gains and losses from investing the next five to 10 years of my life in this venture? Is it right for me and my situation?"*

5. *"Do I sense that this is the right opportunity to seize?"*

6. *"Do I anticipate greater benefit from five years in a startup compared to five years in an established corporation?"*

8. Decision Variables

Mark needed to define the variables that would help him come to a final decision. These variables were the passion that he felt for the startup, whether he could shore up family finances, and the extent of the mindset shift he would have to undergo.

Passion: Mark did not look for a startup; nevertheless, he ran into one. Mark initially mooted the idea of joining a startup because Silicon Valley had made him wary of the startup environment, and the first step in his decision-making process required a significant mind shift. Why did he want to join a startup in the first place? Was it to broaden his managerial responsibilities, his problem-solving skills, or to incubate new technology to benefit the human race? Identifying what he hoped to get out of the experience fundamentally helped him find the right startup. Mark's attraction to a startup was not love at first sight. He used his experience and curiosity to confirm his instincts and passion.

Family finances: Mark had joined a big tech company after graduation. He did not have to worry about the company's revenue, profit, and competitive landscape because the market was proven. Moreover, public companies are governed well because they are in the public eye. A startup, however, was a gamble. Mark had to do his own research and talking to the CEO and the people inside the startup was the right choice. The financial data were not publicly available, so Mark had to ask the founders questions directly to draw his own conclusions as to where the company was on the growth curve. Mark knew the trade-offs he was making. He made the choice to lower his income for greater financial gain down the road.

Mindset shift: Mark saw his value in the startup, and that made him a desirable candidate. His knowledge proved valuable, but he had to take on general work at the startup and fill any gaps. His job description was not defined because roles and responsibilities were ambiguous.

Mark ultimately joined *SuperTech*. He could have chosen to join the next startup because not all startups are the same. Which one is right for an individual requires research.

Mark felt more comfortable as a potential employee after spending personal time with the team. Some startups might only have a few people. They may start in a garage, and other team members might join only when an IPO is imminent. Mark did not pay attention to other startups. Instead, he tried the product and used his own judgment. He believed at the time that there were enough startups that he could join where he could build on top of the initial product. His personal preference was to use the startup as a springboard to leap forward in a context where the company needed him, and he could contribute to its success. More importantly, he needed a startup that would force him to undergo a mindset shift.

Summary

Whether to join a startup is a question many Asian immigrants ask themselves when they look for a job. But it was also a question that Mark found difficult to answer. He pondered joining a good startup many times. Would it jumpstart his career? Would it provide more balance? Mark focused on a specific opportunity when it presented itself and did the research. He talked to friends and family and soul-searched to decide whether that job was right for him. Just like an investor, Mark knew that his time was money. But the decision to join a startup is not as simple as the decision to invest in properties or the stock market. Why should he invest his time in this company?

PART III.

ACHIEVING RHYTHMIC GROWTH

MAX'S STORY

"Keep your Linkedin profile updated; you won't be there long."
Max's friend alerted him right after his first week at HiFintech.

Max Li had been a key Cloud architect for a product line at his previous company. He overcame the language barriers in the early years of his career by taking business language courses and personalized English language coaching. Because of his AWS Cloud technical skills, he was headhunted and hired as a multiple team manager by a competitor.

A friend of Max, who worked for the new firm, gave him some unwarranted advice. His friend warned Max to keep his resume updated because Max's new boss, the VP of Engineering Operations, had a reputation for being extremely demanding and expecting top results with measurable KPIs (key performance indicators).

Max was well-organized, logical, and capable. Once he was in his new position, the VP of Operations used a Slack message to Max and asked him to provide a thirty-day plan and a review at the end of the quarter. The VP wanted to see certain deliverables. Max realized that his boss was indeed demanding. He worked hard to deliver the short-term results that his manager asked for while also devising strategies for long-term initiatives. Max's communication reached new levels as his English vocabulary expanded, and he adapted to the culture, power, and influence of a purely American-managed corporate office.

As a mid-level manager, Max noticed that his teams were more siloed and isolated than he would like them to be. They used cookie-cutter process cycles. Remote work was a large part of day-to-day operations, and Max decided that the company's existing collaboration tool was hindering team creativity and productivity. He collected data on how people collaborated and prepared a report to show how a new collaboration tool would improve team results and ultimately boost the company's bottom line.

Max presented his proposal to his boss in a meeting after bringing up the subject in previous one-on-ones. The VP asked tough questions about budgets, cost savings, and trade-offs. Although the collaboration tool would change the way the teams functioned, the VP did not consider it something that would bring in revenue directly and was against investing in the idea.

Max continued to push for his proposal in subsequent one-on-ones with his boss, linking the problems with existing bottlenecks caused by legacy system tools. Max explained the pros and cons of the current situation and how his proposed system would be of benefit.

After another presentation and tough negotiation, Max's boss approved the proposal. Once the new tool was installed, and its value was realized, Max found that his manager was approving more of his ideas, including bleeding-edge initiatives on machine learning with the largest investments the company had ever committed to in operations. Max was adding maximum value to his company by leveraging his relationships. At one point, he told his boss,

"I have unique problem-solving approaches. I am engineering minded. I can deliver what you want, but I want you to judge me on the results more than the process."

Max had managed to win the support of his new boss within four months, despite a questionable beginning, by using measured communication and a systematic approach. With the total support and trust of his boss, he was now a powerful influencer.

9. Managing the Boss

Max viewed the relationship with his manager as absolutely his responsibility. It might not be harmonious (some personalities do clash), but he could always find ways to make the relationship constructive. He connected with his boss by presenting him with facts and using negotiation. He created a mutual foundation of trust. Fundamentally, Max knew his managers did not have time to focus on getting the details themselves. All managerial decisions were based on his data, and they trusted him. Thus, his management's decisions were based on trust.

———

During one-on-one meetings, Max proposed ideas to his manager. At the next staff meeting, Max's manager presented one of the ideas as his own. This was awkward and upsetting for Max. His jaw dropped, but he later found the strength to praise his manager for a great presentation. Max observed this type of behavior as common practice for some of the managers in the company as well as people in other teams.

———

By providing an idea, Max supported his manager one hundred percent and without any objections. Why? Because by working as a team, he received sponsorships and approvals that granted his idea further access to the next level. The higher an idea goes, the more powerful the decision, and the more impact that person will have on the organization, the individuals, and the product directions. Even though his boss might own one of Max's ideas, Max would rise in influence along with his boss because of their relationship—they are a team.

How do leaders make decisions? They make decisions based on data from their team members. Most senior managers rely on their reports to gather data that the team members deliver along with extensive analysis by trusted individuals. Therefore, managers and leaders ultimately make decisions based on the trust they have in their reports. Max built his relationship with his boss by delivering reliable data. He built mutual trust. Max did not complain when his ideas were claimed by his boss.

10. Owning the Manager-Report Relationship

Max volunteered to take on new initiatives, and he became someone his manager could rely on. He did what mattered the most to align with the management direction. He pivoted his behavior to fit with his manager's personality and characteristics. For example, in order to get the best out of his meeting, Max would go out of his way to ensure his boss would be in an accepting mood. Knowing that his boss normally drank a Coke at two o'clock every day after lunch, Max brought him a Coke when they happened to meet at that hour.

Alignment with his boss and the corporate direction was Max's priority as a middle manager. Additionally, there is significant shuffling and reorganization in big tech companies, and Max stayed out of his silo so that he could engage in the core of the business. He adjusted his objectives on a weekly basis and often asked his manager "Am I aligned?" in one-on-one meetings.

Agile methodology calls for a retrospective every sprint, where the team reviews progress in terms of project expectations. Max followed this practice and held retrospectives monthly and quarterly, even weekly. If the direction of work changed, he followed up with his managers to find out what he should start to do, what he should keep doing, and what he should stop doing.

The illustration below is taken from Angela Duckworth's book "Grit." It shows that the goals of managers at each level are linked. In Max's case, managers broke down the quarterly objectives from one level up into daily activities so that the team members could make sure their work aligned with the manager's goals.

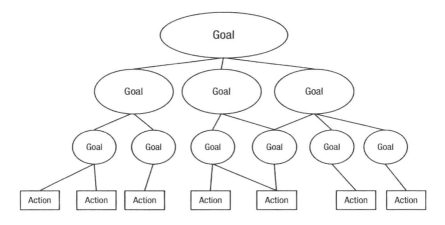

Figure 2 Goals of managers at each level.
Source: Duckworth, *Grit: The Power of Passion and Perseverance*, 2016

11. Managing Up, Across, and Around

Max achieved rhythmic growth by acting as if he was the CEO of his own career. He imagined that he would manage all the relationships that surrounded him as a virtual company. Max managed the relationships regardless of how he felt about the people involved. He needed to manage these people well. He managed up, across, and around depending on his priorities. Max built relationships to manage his boss, his boss's boss, his peers, his team members, and his indirect reports as if they were his personal network.

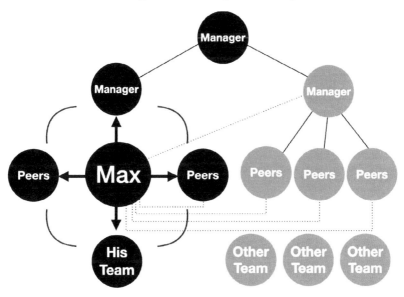

Figure 3 illustrates this relationship management.

12. The Three Pillars of Managing Up

Max was a middle level manager; his manager was a director who reported to a VP under the CEO. To Max, managing up meant managing his director, managing his VP, and even managing the CEO. Max's goals were threefold: to influence the conversation, to educate his boss, and to prep his boss for negotiation.

Influence. Max often prepped his management by making sure his immediate director had the information she needed to do her job. Management makes decisions, and at an elevated level, managers have other information that the lower level is not privy to. Max's director communicated this information and the data that Max provided to her peers and the VP in advance of their discussions. Max often anticipated the issues that would be discussed. The director relied on Max to do the groundwork and to provide solutions.

Education. Max educated his director by providing all the data needed to be fully aware of the issues and the rich data behind them. Because of his efforts, upper management was adequately prepared to consider any solutions that were brought to the table. Max was an expert, and he educated the management by giving them the right information at the right time.

Preparing for Negotiation. Max's director was well-prepared for negotiation because of the trusted data and information Max provided. Max always delivered the most current reports and highlighted the salient findings. The strong relationship between Max and his director meant that management was more likely to approve of his suggestions and discuss them with the executive management team. In turn, Max had a direct impact on decision making within the organization.

———————

Max volunteered as coach for his son's school soccer team. His son, as a second-generation American, was very different from Max. In one game, there was a play where Max's son did not like the referee's call. He began to argue with the ref. Even though the whole team supported his son, Max benched him for the next game. He told his son: "the team is your priority, not the ref's calls. The team needs you to focus on the next play instead of spending valuable time debating with the ref on the field. Your time should be spent bringing the team together to reach the goal, which is to win the game."

———————

Max valued the team more than his own personal satisfaction. He managed his work and tried to instill similar values in his children.

13. Managing Peers

*F*ew *people relish the idea of managing their peers. Managing peers was tough if unprepared. As Alan learned when he was appointed to a manager position, he realized that his peers have substantial influence. Alan learned this as he moved up the corporate ladder and his peers provided feedback on his work. Alan, as a new manager, was careful to maintain good relations with his peers and influence them to smooth his entry into a management role.*

After Alan's promotion to manager was announced in a morning staff meeting, Max organized a social coffee break to celebrate. Alan then faced a difficult choice. At one table sat his old peers while, at another, sat Max with the management. Should Alan sit and chat with his old peers or Max and the senior management? Alan's old peers might find it awkward if he sat with them because now, he was their manager and the dynamics had changed. On the other hand, if Alan sat with the management group, his old peers might feel snubbed. Which group did Alan choose?

Alan chose the best option for this dilemma. He said hello to his new management peers and then sat with his old peers. When it came to managing his old peers, Alan set the tone of the new relationship and was firm and confident from the outset. Alan could always meet his friends after work, but he managed the team, his work, and guided his reports like the North star.

Building a Team: Max continued his career path and moved to another company where he sought promotion opportunities. These opportunities presented themselves more often as he better understood his communication ecosystem. In his new work environment, Max managed multiple teams. As a new member of the organization and, as an outsider, Max's challenge had been to build a team of his own by promoting from the inside.

Max promoted Alan as one of his managers, Alan was a high-potential key talent and worked for a different group. The input from the managers was critical to Alan's promotion because there was a short-list for promotions discussed at the manager meetings.

Alan influenced his own promotion by identifying who was responsible for promotion decisions and who he should talk to about his work. It was not always his direct line manager. In this case, it was Max, a diagonal upper-level manager, who had the most influence on his career. He knew that Max was integral to his nomination for promotions. Socializing with a colleague who had just been promoted, Alan consulted for her advice. He was very grateful to have her support: how she had earned the promotion, who she spoke to, and who championed for her. Alan was aware of who the decision makers were and requested them for feedback during collaboration on projects. He planned his strategy following the path to promotion referencing his colleague.

Alan bridged with team members in neighboring departments, supported those team members, and brought them to the attention of management. In doing so, Alan was noticed by his diagonal manager, Max. Alan had left a good impression with Max because he championed his colleagues. The result was that Max, in turn, championed Alan, and the management group were impressed by Alan's performance. It was an easy decision for Max to support Alan's promotion with the promotion committee because Alan had deftly managed his relationships up, across, and around.

———————

Alan advanced by managing the most influential component of his career, his relationship with *his* boss. Max, for his part, had built a supportive team that included Alan. The team lifted Max up instead of dragging him down. Max learned how to convert those who were working against him into his supporters. The whole team was like a barge in a lock in a canal. By working as one on team projects, they all rose together to reach the next level. Then, they celebrated small victories as they gradually reached milestones.

THE MIDDLE MANAGEMENT DILEMMA

Middle managers face conflicts on many fronts. They must make sure that what the teams are doing aligns with the corporate direction, and they must balance the available resources.

Alignment: Max often checked with his boss on the overall corporate direction. Then, in turn, he aligned his teams and his second-in-command, Alan. Max found correlations in the form of shared goals. Many teams had different priorities and deadlines, and at times they conflicted with the other peer groups. By finding common goals with colleagues, Max collaborated to achieve those goals. Even in a conflict situation, he found shared goals. Sharing victories with colleagues was a great experience even if they were not necessarily his favorite friends.

Getting Projects Done: There are three main components that contribute to the success of any project: human resources, time, and money. The three components are closely linked. In any situation, one or two can yield the third. How middle management balances these three components is often a good indicator of how successful a middle manager can be in making the right tradeoffs at the right time.

———————

Max had a good grasp of his budget situation. At the beginning of the year, he had a full budget to spend, whereas at the end of the fiscal year, he had to manage tight budget constraints. If he didn't pace things well, he would have to juggle resources and deadlines. Max's supervisor set deadlines, but Max was proactive and communicated what he needed to meet those deadlines well in advance to avoid any project hold-ups. He explained any tradeoffs that would result because of budget limitations.

When Max found himself with plenty of money and a looming deadline, he doubled up on manpower with the right individuals and consultants, whatever he needed to get the project done. Max figured out how to maximize the resources available to him and align his results with the expectations of the VP of operations.

In some cases, Max took on projects but was not exactly sure what they would entail. In these cases, he talked to Alan and his team, who researched and consulted with other experts. The team found the best individuals internally and externally to help them spearhead these tough projects. By bringing in a new set of experts and finding answers, Max became a more technical and better overall manager.

Max and his team drafted a project plan to move forward. He identified all the priorities, decided what steps to take first, and built in enough of a buffer to allow for the unknowns. Top management demanded real-time data and results, so Max made sure he was not putting himself in a difficult spot by overreaching. Max planned his resources carefully, which also meant preventing his team from burning out by efficiently spreading out work, building in milestone celebrations, in the form of cocktail events and coffee socials, and pro-viding staff with downtime.

Middle management required Max to first align his organiza-tion with the corporate goals and manage the team to get the work done. Max realized that all his daily affairs centered around commu-nicating with people.

14. The Art of Employee-to-Manager Communication

*D*uring the COVID-19 pandemic, team structures and ways of working changed. Rightsizing teams, or streamlining, became prevalent. Companies were forced to cut costs, and employees were particularly affected because of remote working. After Alan was promoted, he rebuilt his team. One of his new hires was Vivi. She learned the hard way how important it is to perform the right way, which is to stay connected with her management under all circumstances.

Vivi started a new job just as her new office was shutting down because of the remote working arrangement caused by the COVID-19 pandemic. Her team and all employees were to work remotely. Vivi completed her orientation and was set up at home to do her tasks. However, for the initial three months, Vivi was an introverted, qualified quiet. She attended meetings when Alan called, but she felt lost never meeting a single person in the office. She was doing all she could to learn and all that Alan, her manager, asked of her. However, Alan heard nothing from Vivi. It was clear from the system that Vivi was entering tasks, but she was not reaching out in any way. Vivi's team members didn't know her either; she was not visible, or her discreet behavior became a red flag in Alan's view.

Vivi was doing her work, performing demos when asked, and attending virtual meetings. This would be meeting expectations under normal working circumstances and would not be a cause for concern. However, because of the remote working conditions during the pandemic, the dynamics and expectations had changed. When the company was right-sized, Vivi was at a disadvantage.

Regardless of the pandemic, working remotely is becoming a global norm. People who make an extra effort to check in with the team and their boss on a regular basis shift normal working rules and habits, and Vivi should have done the same. She could even have gone the extra mile and initiated virtual meetings to discuss issues. Working remotely requires extra effort to stay visible or connected to compensate for the lack of office presence under the unusual pandemic conditions.

As an individual contributor, Vivi was learning how to navigate a giant American corporation. As a Chinese American, Vivi learned that employee-manager communication comprised much more than daily task delivery. By observing Max, Alan, and Vivi, as a first generation-immigrant can learn how to leap forward using communication in the corporate world.

15. Communicate, Communicate, Communicate

Max illustrated the best approach to employee-manager and manager-employee communication. He showed how the report can take responsibility for the relationship so that it is a constructive one for everyone involved.

Social Media

Max understood how his boss preferred to communicate. For example, he knew that his manager had a WeChat account, but rarely logged into WeChat, so Max used Slack and company-approved messaging systems. He used a variety of ways to communicate so that his messages didn't become boring or annoying. He used an appropriate communication style and timing that was consistent and habitual. He stayed connected and checked in at least every three days.

Max used tools that were familiar to his manager to communicate. He even used the tools that his boss preferred, and he also considered the timing of any communications. He did not send messages to his manager at dinner time because they could be overlooked or forgotten. By doing that, he respected his boss's communication preferences and personal time. Social media and messaging is fast and convenient, but it is also easy to abuse. Knowing his manager's preferred style, Max could effectively deliver the information his manager needed.

Max connected with his boss on a regular basis. He had a conversation with her every three days or so. If Max did not have some type of contact every three days with his manager, it could be interpreted as a red flag.

Many people, particularly those from Asian-American cultures, tend to wait for their managers to approach them when there is an issue, but this does not work in their favor. If Max's manager had to ask him a question, Max would assume that he had not prepared his boss adequately or provided the information she needed.

One-on-one Meetings

One-on-one meetings are bidirectional, in other words, top down and bottom up. One-on-ones help senior management to detail the tasks needed to complete objectives through top-down interactions, but they also pinpoint escalating issues and roadblocks on the front line from bottom up interactions.

Max used his one-on-one meetings with his manager strategically. He steered his manager and the team in the right direction by preparing three key points for discussion in his one-on-ones. He took note of every conversation, email, or message on Slack that he received from his boss, and, in turn, kept management in the loop of key activities. Max sent his boss FYI notes so that she was always aware of what Max planned to discuss in his meetings. He leveraged every touch point and raised issues in his messaging so that he associated solution options ready in advance of his one-on-one meetings with his boss.

Max used his one-on-ones to prepare his boss for upcoming decisions or meetings with others. Many decisions were made ahead of critical meetings so that there were no surprises, and the decisions made were well-informed and based on reliable data. After Max presented the information needed to his boss, the meetings were elevated as a rubber-stamp on already established decisions. Details, such as who was going to do a task, how many people would be needed, and when a task needed to be done, were settled well in advance of key meetings.

Prioritizing a List for Each One-on-one Meeting

One-on-one meetings can become an opportunity to go through a laundry list of items, but that serves little purpose.

Max managed Alan and other direct reports by using his one-on-one meetings with them as coaching sessions. When Alan was first promoted as a new manager, he was anxious. His emotions were impacted by the result of his one-on-one meetings with Max. Alan was careful to follow the management directions. He gradually matured into his position by always preparing two key points for his discussions with Max.

Max gave Alan some guidelines for their one-on-one meetings. Alan followed the guidelines choosing only the most important items to discuss. He prepared just two or three subjects for discussion. He made sure the subjects were interesting, critical things that Max would consider a priority and that he would want to hear about.

Alan tried a few different strategies for his one-on-one meetings with his manager. Sometimes he presented a laundry list of issues, but the impression it left on Max was that he appeared to be playing defense and not proactively foreseeing potential issues. Alan seemed to be doing the minimum instead of taking his work to the next level. As a manager, going through a laundry list of issues would lead management to think that what Alan presented was not that important. Alan stayed with his strategy of only bringing up two items for discussion in his one-on-ones with Max.

If Max did not have time for a one-on-one with Alan, Alan would follow-up with an email that listed the points. That way, Max was aware of the pressing issues requiring attention. When it comes to promotion, managers look for people who can take responsibility beyond their current position. If Alan only took care of his immediate issues rather than attacking issues as a self-starter, this would be considered a weakness, and Alan would not be a candidate for promotion to the next level of management.

Staying Connected

In today's digital world, information is exploding. Max observed that new information would come from all angles—from his peer group, from first line management and from executive management. Being the center of the information flow was complicated. Max understood that staying connected was very different from simply not being distant. Avoiding the problem of distance can be resolved by a post in a group chat or attending virtual meetings even as a fly on the wall. Max's position was a one-to-many relationship. Max, however, maintained many one-to-one relationships.

———————

Max found opportunities to provide relevant information to his boss so that decisions could be made in advance of critical meetings. Many Asian Americans love to stage a final unveiling or deliver a surprise during a team meeting, but the unexpected is not easy for a manager to handle. A manager must always act in the best interests of all stakeholders, and that requires careful consideration of available data in advance, not surprises.

Max raised issues before they became a problem. Keeping his boss involved meant that she became part of the team and was always fully informed. Max's boss had a circle of conversations that he was not aware of, but she relied on the information that he provided to have constructive conversations. That allowed his company to respond, pivot when necessary, and avoid a disaster.

Raising Issues with Options for a Solution

Max knew that problems are easy to find, but what is difficult is finding a top-notch solution. There are many options for a solution, but none are a slam dunk. It takes persistence and relentlessness to find that single great solution. Max had to be driven to reach that one ideal solution but flexible enough to give up all the other options even if it meant going back to the drawing board because early thoughts and assumptions were wrong. Max had to change things, and solving problems took adaptation. It took a lot of hard work to find a simple answer that the customer would like to a complex enterprise problem.

———————

Max's leadership consisted of foreseeing problems but providing options for solutions is where the strength of middle management lies. Upper management needed data to solve problems holistically, and they also needed solution options to make tradeoffs with customer priorities. Management does not have the time to explore the details of the solutions. For that, management relies on middle managers like Max. Moreover, if Max only provided one solution, his boss would counter with other scenarios. As a mid-level manager, Max navigated by suggesting the top first solution, then the top second solution, and then the third solution. This strategy demonstrated the leadership skills and maturity that are the essence of middle management. It was also an approach that prevented costly bottlenecks.

On the contrary, some managers raise issues and ask their manager questions. A manager might respond well in that circumstance, but the team must move forward instead of dwelling on questions. If Max had chosen this approach, the impact on the team would be one of hindrance rather than moving things forward. Max successfully solved problems for his boss, which helped to funnel him from middle management to upper management.

Celebrating Small Victories

Taking time to celebrate success stamps an exclamation mark on a project well done. Teams and peer groups remember these moments. It's equally as important to celebrate small victories by hosting a coffee social or a cocktail hour.

Max organized and created celebratory events between projects for his team and management. He talked about successes in meetings to draw attention to the team's achievements. This solidified the team and encouraged positive conversation across teams.

Max praised both his own team and the teams he worked with on cross-functional projects, bringing them to the attention of upper management. Max alerted diagonal upper managers if somebody under their leadership did a great job. That way, he made an impression and influenced his peer group.

Praising Your Team

As a manager, Max conducted one-on-ones with his team members. Max shaped a pattern for his one-on-one meetings that always started with something positive. He kept notes and highlighted and praised the individual, told them where they exceeded expectations, and then listened carefully to what they had to say about weekly tasks. At the end, Max always closed by saying thank you.

In Asian culture, it is common to praise the whole team over any individual. It may sometimes seem at odds culturally to praise somebody or appreciate someone's work in a meeting. However, Asian American managers who reach out of their comfort zone culturally in the western environment bridge the gap in a diverse employee group. Realizing that there is a need to praise whenever there is an opportunity to collaborate builds stronger work relationships every day. By praising his staff, Max's positive action impacted his personal power and his relationship power.

Max praised his own team and celebrated success with other teams after the completion of a cross-functional project. He told his diagonal upper-level manager that their team had done an outstanding job. These habits are particularly critical with peer relationships because connecting to peer group meetings does not happen regularly.

During manager meetings, Max's boss received positive feedback from the upper peer group of diagonal managers. Later, when Max proposed a key initiative to the upper management group for additional funding, the diagonal upper-level manager was a strong advocate of that proposal. Thus, Max had a champion who could support him in addition to his own manager. This would have even more impact on Max's next promotion.

Getting to Know a Manager's Personal Network

Max was aware of his boss's network and with whom she had a close working relationship. He was aware of her business connections, which was something he learned through experience. For example, Max was invited to attend a senior staff meeting where he was exposed to a whole new level of management relationships that were shadowed by his manager's influence. Max must support his direct manager as well as his manager's interest network. To do that, he must be aware of who might have a vested interest in a project or issue.

———

Physical personal networks are as important as professional networks. Executives socialize on weekends in the same way that Asians visit their families and friends, engage in cultural and family activities, shop at Chinese grocery stores, and eat at Chinese restaurants. By being aware of his manager's networks, Max was able to have a third eye over the business grapevine beyond his own traditional Chinese siloed friends.

Summary

Managing communication is an art. At most, Max probably had twenty minutes each week to sit with his boss for discovery. Knowing his boss's expectations was critical to him. Knowing what resources, he needed and planning how to get them were critical for Max. Otherwise, he would have been flying blind.

Just as Max needed a clear view of his own situation, he also needed a clear view of his manager's situation. Max understood his boss's pain points in order to execute his daily tasks and remove the impediments to their resolution. He mapped out where he fit in his manager's context to identify the shared goals, map out his role, and then act as the implementer.

Max became the implementer of the management's agenda. He became the eye and the hand of upper management. He executed what mattered the most and reported back with data. Max was always ready to pivot when management called for change. Remember, a manager is privy to information at a higher level, and their reports do not see this information. Thus, the reason for their decisions is not always immediately evident

For Max, it was easy to identify the key management relationships, but it was difficult to turn the relationship into a successful one under the political environment. There are many steps between identifying political relationships and building a smooth connection. It took personality and cultural understanding to follow through and build influence and trust. Max had to be consistent when presenting his vision and flexible to adapt to his manager's style. He needed to be persistent to build a relationship with his boss. He also needed to be flexible in pursuing it because some of the early thoughts and assumptions were not true. He had to change things. It takes adaptation for middle management to be successful, and it takes hard work to be a middle manager that people trust and respect.

PART IV.

THE MOVE TO BEIJING

KEVIN'S STORY

A man with kind eyes and a humble smile held up a sign:

"BEIJING WELCOMES YOU! Kevin UA 889"

Kevin found his pick-up driver at Beijing International airport. Kevin was so excited to return to Beijing as an expatriate. He couldn't wait to start his new assignment, even though his wife and children had stayed behind in San Francisco. It had been a long journey in the making, and it had started like this ...

Kevin was a senior IT manager for a fast-growing e-commerce company. He commuted by ferry from Bainbridge Island to his office in Seattle. The view of downtown Seattle as the ferry approached was usually obscured by thick fog, and the chilly air would be enough to keep the passengers inside, tapping on laptops or checking their phones. But there were some days when the approach to the city took Kevin's breath away. The sun would shine brilliantly, low in a pure blue sky. The Seattle skyline would stand out sharp and strong against the blue sky and the turquoise Pacific Ocean. Tall silver skyscrapers glinted glasslike as they reflected the morning rays. Out on the deck, the smell of the Northwest Pacific Northwest forest combined with the ocean water awakened all of Kevin's senses, and the crisp air stimulated his mind to marvel at the clarity around him. On those mornings, Kevin had a crystal-clear view of the city as he made his way to his office. Kevin longed for as clear a view of his situation at work as he had of downtown Seattle on those rare, fresh mornings. He needed to get rid of the fog that wouldn't clear in his mind. Kevin was concerned with his professional growth and the next steps in his career. He was considering a return to China.

16. The Four Situations

*K*evin *worked at a huge e-commerce conglomerate as an IT infra-structure professional. He was involved in all types of business situations, and his work was extremely complex. His functional area gave him a holistic view with a unique snapshot of the business's growth. Kevin was involved in early-stage initiatives, fast-growing projects, and mature cash cows all operating under the big tech company's portfolio. Each of these business contexts called for different management strategies and frameworks.*

———————

Kevin observed four common business situations: startups, fast growth, adaptation, and cash cows.

1. The Startup

Every new initiative within a big corporation is a startup situation. It will have the same characteristics as a pure startup but with some nuances. Kevin's role was to provide internal third-party infrastructure and IT support to the startup projects within his company. In addition, these startup projects also required financing, human resources, legal, leadership, sponsor, and technology services. The most recent startup that Kevin was observing was a new e-commerce pharmacy division, which faced the typical issues of any startup:

- The startup needed people.

- The startup needed a clean slate to begin work.

- The startup needed a strategy, structure, and systems.

Most important for the startup scenario is building the right team and getting the talent to architect the technology front end and back end; a startup requires a group of people who are focused and energetic. A startup also needs a clean slate. There should be no hangovers or baggage to stall momentum or take it in the wrong direction. Lastly, a startup needs structure and systems so that the team can function without spending valuable time on the wrong things. Any deviation can mean that the startup might have to restart from scratch.

Kevin noticed that it was easy to have ideas. Big tech companies have no end of new ideas to explore in incubators but turning ideas into successful products is where the magic lies. There were a lot of steps between an idea and a product. It takes persistence and relentlessness to be successful. Stakeholders have to be stubborn about the vision and flexible in pursuing it. Responsibility should lie with a single accountable person who is confident enough to pivot if early thoughts and assumptions seem wrong. It takes adaptation to make a

*vision successful and a ton of hard work to make a product that people
will love.*

2. Fast Growth

The second type of situation that Kevin observed was rapid
growth. The competitive e-commerce company had acquired a retail
shoe platform to accommodate its fast growth in the shoe market space. During this period, the organization had rapidly added
resources because there was fierce competition from other e-commerce sectors. The whole e-commerce industry was in fast-growth
mode, and resources would soon be hard to come by. Decisions
had to be made quickly in this context; otherwise, growth would be
delayed if a company moved too late in the game.

Kevin observed the following challenges for the fast-growing
e-commerce shoe platform:

> – Fast growth required a strong business structure and
> systems.

> – Fast growth meant growing pains.

> – Fast growth called for rapid scale-up.

The fast growth scenario called for systems and structure to
ensure direction and order. Without structure to act as guardrails,
people quickly fall out of alignment when things are moving fast. A

lack of alignment stymies creativity, results, and growth. Also, fast growth cannot continue without the monetization of a product, so leaders must ensure control while quickly expanding the initiative.

3. Adaptation

In an adaptation situation, an organization evolves to take on new challenges. Many established businesses reach the status quo and become stagnant. Companies or initiatives in adaptation must reinvent themselves and re-orient toward a new direction to prevent failure.

Adaptation occurs in normal circumstances. It's a natural part of the project cycle. But adaptation also occurs under extraordinary circumstances. For example, during the COVID-19 epidemic, the healthcare and IT sectors responded rapidly to the need for health tracking software. Those countries that were able to control the devastating impact of the pandemic and continue pursuing innovations in the health space thrived. Taiwan and Singapore experienced seismic growth during the pandemic because they were able to control the impact of the virus.

Kevin observed the following challenges for adaptation within his company:

– Adaptation required a mindset switch.

– Leaders had to refocus and reshape their thinking and their teams' thinking.

– The leader and the team had to evolve.

– The "rest and vest" factor.

In the adaptation scenario, all stakeholders need to change their mindset for things to reshape and evolve. Such sudden change is stressful, and the hands-on teams must be in a good place in terms of work-life balance to be able to focus and re-orient to the task at hand without distractions. Under adaptation, there is typically little opportunity for professional advancement because there is minimal movement among personnel. With adaptation, the boat has already sailed, and people are firmly in their seats. In fact, managers tend to remain in their positions for a long time. This dynamic is the "rest and vest" factor, when managers stay in their comfortable management roles to maintain the status quo.

Ultimately, the goal of adaptation is to transition a failing project to profitability, and that is quite the challenge.

4. Cash Cows

Cash cows are mature projects in danger of imminent failure either due to competition or customer trends. With cash cows, there is a need to re-engage everybody involved to plan for future modifications. In this context, the next generation product needs to be revived, repackaged, or introduced. The leader must be in "ready, aim, shoot" mode. Kevin observed that stakeholders must be reenergized, the leader must make difficult choices and initiate change, and time is short.

However, the first step is reorganization, and that takes time and is stressful for everyone. Reorganization may mean letting people and projects go, which is hard, and particularly so when there are time pressures. However, if action is not taken quickly, the problem will not be fixed. Whatever it takes to reverse an unsatisfactory trajectory must be done methodically, and the leader has to make those difficult decisions.

There is a lot of baggage in this scenario. The leader must launch a new product, but there is no clean slate as there is with a startup, and customers, employees, culture, systems, all come along. Reenergizing calls for a heroic effort by the leader.

Kevin observed the following challenges for cash cows within his company:

- There must be change, but in what form?

- Change must occur quickly before the cash cow fails.

- Cash cows come with baggage.

17. The Relocation

Abig corporation might be iconic in one space, but they also seek to expand their business to other business areas or geographic locations like China. They have amazing track records and proven ability to produce new technologies and disruptive innovation. Kevin observed startups, fast growth, adaptation, and cash cows concurrently, and his portfolio of work was complicated, supporting all business situations.

———————

Having worked on e-commerce initiatives for 10 years, Kevin's career had plateaued. He was at a loss about his career growth. He was eyeing the possibility of a director or VP position, but the language requirements shattered his confidence. So far, his Chinese language skills had never been used in his career, so he started to consider a move to China.

Coming off an annual review, Kevin had done a fantastic job; such a fantastic job that his boss told him "just carry on doing what you have been doing for the last few years." Kevin perceived that there was little opportunity for growth in his current role.

As a middle-aged man with a family, Kevin was feeling the pressure to reach the pinnacle of his career. He learned of the rapid growth that China had been experiencing since the 90s; meanwhile, Kevin went from home to work and then home again every day feeling unfulfilled. Urban Seattle life seemed stagnant. He would listen to the news and hear that Silicon Valley companies were setting up offices in China to take advantage of the country's economic momentum.

Kevin went to a XueYuan Lu event with the Beijing University Alumni Association. For the event, the family flew to China, and the children had the opportunity to meet their grandparents in Beijing. At the event, Kevin was excited to see that his classmates were already making significant contributions to the Chinese economy in the IT, infrastructure, and construction industries, and Kevin was convinced that he should somehow be a part of that. He concluded that for his career to advance, he must find an opportunity to return to Beijing with his western working experience.

Kevin first gingerly unveiled the idea of returning to Beijing to his wife, Grace, and then his children. Grace, who also graduated from Beijing University, was in full support. She was excited at the prospect of being back with her parents and siblings, for her children to meet their cousins, and for them to learn the Chinese language.

———

Kevin and his wife discussed the challenges and implications of a move to China to advance Kevin's career. Moving a family of five from North America to Beijing was quite an undertaking, and there were lots of questions to answer.

- Could the family remain a unit?

- If the whole family moved, how long would the family stay in China, and in which city would they choose to settle?
- How often should they return to the United States to maintain connections and to keep up their children's English education.
- How would they meet the needs of each family member? For example, should Kevin's wife give up her job in the United States, and how would her career be affected if she did?
- How would the children's education be managed? Kevin had one child in elementary school, a kindergartner, and a toddler.
- How would the family finance the move? Should the house in the United States be sold or rented out? What would be the cost-of-living implications of a move to Beijing?

It was easy for Kevin and Grace to think about going back to Beijing because they were originally from Beijing. But their children had never been there, could not speak Chinese, and lacked a well-rounded Western and Chinese education. In addition, there were overwhelming logistics involved in a move to Beijing. Kevin needed his family's support. He needed a plan that he could stick to so that he would not give up. Even though the family agreed to move, Kevin and Grace had to adapt to make the return to Beijing for the whole family successful.

18. Landing in Beijing

*A*fter a series of honest and frank discussions, the family agreed that a move to China would be exciting. Kevin explored possible company initiatives in China. He also considered founding a startup venture in China, but the risks were greater as an independent entrepreneur.

Kevin presented a proposal to his executives for breaking into the Chinese market. The emerging Chinese market was not one the company could ignore, so, within six months, Kevin was given the go ahead to build a new division in Beijing.

One month later, Kevin landed in Beijing to begin preparations to set up a new entity. He was alone in Beijing. Grace remained in the United States with the children to prepare the house for sale.

Kevin found himself in startup mode in a foreign country. He had to build an office from scratch in an unfamiliar environment. He needed to find space, fit it out with IT infrastructure, and find a team. He had little support, and he was not sure what problems he would encounter.

To start with, there were technological differences between Facebook, Amazon, and Google in the United States and JD.com, Alibaba, and Tencent in China. Kevin may have understood the dynamics of a startup, but the practicalities of building a startup in a strange country presented a challenge of a different dimension. Kevin wondered how he would bridge such a digital divide and facilitate operations between headquarters and the regional office.

Kevin first hired a human resource firm to find staff. He also started to look for office locations. He began the registration process for the initiative as a wholly owned foreign entity (WOFE) for a U.S. tech company. Ken was responsible for all the office outfitting and hardware infrastructure. He was the face of finance, marketing, sales, engineering, and operations. Kevin devoted all his time to establishing the office.

There were plenty of initial hiccups. A staffing firm that he hired to find the right team lost all the best candidates to a competitor. A contractor that Kevin hired to fit out the office went over budget and needed constant nudging. There was one problem after another. However, Kevin was determined to get the office up and running before his family arrived in six months.

When Kevin's wife and children arrived, he knew that his schedule would be disrupted, and he would no longer be able to devote all his time to the startup. There would be lots to be done—finding housing, schools, and entertainment for the children. Kevin realized that the sooner his family was settled in Beijing, the sooner he could focus again on the startup. He was now not only racing to build the startup, but he was in a race to build a life for his family.

———

Kevin and his wife both spoke Chinese and were keen for the children to do the same. So, the family chose to live in an exclusively Chinese neighborhood. Unfortunately, the children found the cultural immersion difficult, and finding friends when they did not speak the language took time.

The children also attended a local school where the lessons were all taught in Chinese, it added to the children's discomfort. There were communication difficulties on many fronts. Not only were the children feeling the physical isolation from their friends back home in the United States, but their social media connections also had time zone differences and the lack of real time connection created further gaps with their American social friends online.

Ultimately, Kevin's children transferred to an international school where the curriculum was taught in English. There, they were much happier making new friends. Kevin also encouraged his family to engage in community support services so that his children could connect with local Chinese children. The family donated to an orphanage to show their support for their community.

Kevin took pains to keep in touch with friends and family in the United States. He created a podcast every month or so to keep them updated on the family's news. The family took a trip back to the United States once a year to keep on top of technology trends and to visit with family and friends.

From time to time, Kevin took his children to work to expose them to business culture and to give his wife a break. Soon, however,

Grace began to feel frustrated and unfulfilled. She had made the sacrifice of leaving her job as an AI researcher mentoring PhD students in the United States, and the transition to full-time parenting in Beijing was a difficult one. Only three months ago, she had been on the verge of a breakthrough for an AI robotics model; now, she was navigating the school runs for her children, meeting with school counselors, cooking, cleaning, and coping with a chaotic household. The cumulative stresses on the whole family caused a rift in Kevin and Grace's marriage that was greater than ever before.

19. Securing Resources

Under Kevin's management, the Beijing office thrived. Kevin had indeed succeeded in breaking into the Chinese market, and his company was considering opening other regional offices in Asia.

Kevin's success meant that he would be the person to head a new regional office. Now that he had the experience of building the Beijing office, Kevin had a better idea of what the task entailed and the resources he would need next time. He was careful not to make any moves before first securing the necessary support. Everything had to align with the corporate strategy, and that meant tackling different hurdles in different countries.

Kevin, as the head of a fast-growth entity, needed to make trade-off decisions on behalf of the headquarters. Kevin envisioned the long and short-term goals of any expansion. He listed what resources he would need in order to meet the deadlines. He determined the costs, benefits, and trade-offs.

———————

One year later, the Beijing office was no longer a startup, and it had entered fast-growth mode. Kevin had successfully established the office, and there were already plans to expand the Beijing operation. Kevin had experienced the complexities of middle management. He had built and maintained a busy regional office that supported the overall vision of the headquarters, promoted the achievements of the regional team, and placated upper management and stakeholders.

While Kevin was in China, the COVID-19 pandemic changed the way he worked. Less travel freed up time, and he took advantage of this extra time to engage in additional learning to build skills. Less travel also meant that he lost physical connection with headquarters. However, online Zoom meetings brought access to an even bigger world. Kevin could reach a much wider audience virtually. It was possible to make more connections, talk to more people, to reach out and make things happen.

During the pandemic, Kevin organized virtual lunches, huddled people together, and became the centerpiece of his team. He naturally became a leader, bridging the divide between headquarters and the regional office. When he returned to a more typical work mode post-COVID, his role was a continuation of what he had been doing before only Kevin now had a wider network, he was more visible, and he had more influence.

The COVID-19 pandemic, while it was economically devastating, also brought opportunities. During the pandemic, many companies-initiated diversity and inclusion efforts because other projects were put on hold. Managers need people to head these initiatives, and ideally the leaders of these initiatives are not white males. Thus, diversity and inclusion initiatives are the perfect opportunity for females to lead projects and flex their leadership muscles.

There will continue to be reshuffling and reorganization that will create even more chances for people to shine. This is a good time to be prepared. Always consider what may occur in the future, and how you can take the time to prepare for it as the world moves beyond the pandemic.

20. Ethical Guardianship

As Kevin expanded his team to hundreds of employees, he encountered cultural differences that he had not anticipated. He acted as the intermediary between staff and headquarters to ensure that the U.S company's rules and regulations were upheld. Some of the U.S. rules conflicted with Chinese culture. For example, Chinese workers have a different approach to per diem travel expenses. They often will spend up to their allotted daily allowance even if the expenses are not business-related. This is just an accepted practice in many Chinese companies. However, U.S. companies require receipts, and the per diem cannot be used for personal expenses. There are many similar cultural nuances that make management of foreign workers difficult.

Even though the U.S. corporation provided regular online ethics training as a guide to doing business in China, the realities of operating in a foreign nation were very different. It was Kevin's responsibility to ensure results, particularly in a competitive sales environment, while not contravening his company's ethics. This meant that Kevin often had to terminate a relationship with a vendor who did not meet the high standards of ethics requirements, even if it would be detrimental to Kevin's reputation.

Being the best person, you can be in life is important. People can make shortcuts and sacrifice standards to win because they know how to play the game, but that is short term. Winning a deal with an unethical person is never a good deal and working with unethical individuals is soul destroying. Quality and authenticity are values that stand the test of time.

21. Emotional Independence

Kevin aspired to grow professionally and to reap the material comforts and wealth that executive leadership brings. But there is a less obvious and rarely considered aspect to reaching professional maturity.

As Kevin climbed the corporate ladder, his perspectives and social circles changed. He evolved as a person, and that affected his relationships with others. Some of his close acquaintances remained static, they did not evolve along with him, and Kevin increasingly found himself in a lonely place. He could no longer maintain the same relationships he once had. Some people find the transition from manager to executive difficult because they lose friends and make new ones.

As a senior leader in a large organization, it is isolating and challenging to be the only one making decisions that impact the lives of so many employees. At this level, college classmates who Kevin once confided in and consulted could no longer support him professionally at this new vantage point. Kevin's old network was no longer adequate, and he had to find new advisors and coaches. In his private life, Kevin found new social outlets. Fundamentally, your personal life and your emotions are another aspect of professional growth, but it is an aspect so often overlooked.

22. Influence

Kevin gained positive and political influence by building alliances. Many shadow organizations exist in companies, and these shadow organizations tend to wield the most influence. The shadow organizations dictate the decisions based on position power, leadership power, knowledge power, and product power. The shadow organization, however, is not found on the organization chart.

As the head of a regional office, Kevin was already involved in these influential circles. He understood the politics and began discussions with those who could initiate approval for expansion.

———————

Kevin's expansion involved acquiring a medical firm with headquarters in the United States. He became depressed because the people at headquarters were stymying his efforts in China. Kevin's Chinese revenue had gone up five hundred percent the previous year, which had led to his promotion to regional manager for Asia Pacific. Kevin then had two bosses, one in Seattle and one in Asia Pacific.

Kevin wanted to acquire a company in Japan to boost Japanese revenues and local business operations. The acquisition required headquarter approvals from about thirty different people. Kevin met with all these people from different cross-functions, but he constantly met with resistance. It became clear that there was a conflict between the engineering and marketing groups, and Kevin's project became a bat-tleground for these two departments.

Influence is a soft skill. Having a positive influence was key for Kevin. He realized that it didn't matter how good his proposal was, if he didn't have influence, his proposal would not go through. Kevin figured out who supported him, who was against him, and who was a swing voter. He then used his influence with swing voters to get his proposals through.

Building Alliances

How did Kevin visualize his influencer network? Who helped him to obtain influence? With whom did he collaborate to advance his ideas and processes. What resources did he need? Who did he influence to get those resources?

Kevin realized that once you reach management, your work becomes more people-oriented and less task-oriented. He focused on correlations and influence in certain areas of the organization, not necessarily the whole organization. Building alliances means finding common goals and then staying in alignment. It is not authority. Alliances are the key to influence. Only through alliances can Kevin, first, influence, and second, find resources. By building an alliance with one person, Kevin can then figure out his next alliance and slowly expand his influence. It is a systematic approach to a complex situation.

Summary

During his time in China, Kevin looked at each factor that affected his work individually and then tried to fit the pieces together like a puzzle. Kevin built alliances so that he could secure the support and resources he needed. He also allowed time to focus on his own advancement and make sure he was attending to the needs of his family as well as his company.

Just as Kevin sometimes had a clear view of the city skyline on beautiful sunny mornings on his ferry boat ride to Seattle, he developed the same clear view of his situation while in China.

Although assimilation to China was a challenge for Kevin and his family, building and expanding the office allowed Kevin to grow professionally and personally in the process. Kevin perfected his T-shape. Kevin's T-shape was composed of the technical skills he had been developing for 10 years—for example, his cloud infrastructure knowledge. The horizontal part of his T were his cross-function skills that he developed as he grew into his management director position in China. For example, his management of operations, HR, marketing, and sales. Kevin did not need to be an expert in the horizontal part of his T, he only needed a working knowledge of those areas. Kevin's move to China balanced out his T.

A systematic approach that is based on first obtaining a clear view is more likely to ensure success when taking on a new role. The China experience made Kevin an ideal candidate for his next role as CEO. Years later, Kevin returned to the United States and joined the board as an iconic member.

PART V.

LEAP FORWARD

NANCY'S STORY

Nancy was VP and head of sales for a biotech startup. After earning her PhD in chemistry, she worked in the United States as a scientist. Later, she was relocated to China where she led a team for a Clinical Research Organization (CRO). She was a driving force behind their mission to discover new medicines. The CRO business had momentum in China. More seed funding came in, and Nancy became a promising candidate for CEO, managing hundreds of scientists and many product lines.

The quality of the CRO work was highly valuable. Nancy's task shifted from cost saving to providing global high standard delivery. Everything was going smoothly until Nancy became completely overwhelmed by the tidal wave of information hitting her desk every day. Then, to make matters worse, the head of research and development complained that her management style did not allow him enough latitude to comply with industry standards.

Nancy was a scientist and had worked in the drug discovery space herself. Therefore, she was most familiar with the research and development section and took great interest in its progress. Before she had reached the executive level, Nancy would look at the P&L (profit and loss) and the quarterly finance reports, but she would not attend the investors' meetings. Now, however, as executive head of sales, it was her responsibility to participate in those meetings and to answer journalists' questions. Many of the questions were politically sensitive; for example, the journalists would question her about the ethics of using animals for testing in product discovery.

Nancy embraced the idea that she should act as a role model. She knew that as an executive, she was under the spotlight. She was challenged to manage her time and all of her responsibilities and was overwhelmed by the onslaught of data. It was an anxious moment when navigating the public domain leading to press conferences.

23. Superpowers

Rapid developments in China's commerce and technology have created a whole new generation of C-level executives. These leaders are young, dynamic, and with new ideas and approaches. Developing a C-level mindset was critical to her success. Becoming a top leader is a seismic shift. In her role as VP and potential CEO, Nancy had a handful of direct reports who managed hundreds of scientists and experts of the same domain. Nancy used all her skills to act as the caller of the game instead of a player of the game.

Michelle, who was introduced in the first section of this book, learned to transition her skills because she moved from a familiar environment where she was on the top of her game to one where she was a beginner all over again. Like a professional table tennis player who wants to become a tennis player, she had to work hard to attain the form and muscle memory needed for tennis. Nancy, on the other hand, had already perfected the art of tennis.

At this level, Nancy's emphasis was on influencing decisions and building correlations because the decisions made at the executive level have consequences for hundreds of company projects and the thousands of people working on them. Correlation and influence, therefore, are superpowers of the C-level mindset.

Many people like Nancy assume that success depends on the people that they know, but that is not necessarily all true. Nancy's team supported her, and her peers were behind her, but these individuals represent the few small circles that Nancy interacts with daily. At the C-level, it is harder to reach people in a broader sense. Much of Nancy's success depended on the people that she managed. Although she would not succeed in winning over everyone, finding shared goals was the best path to influence a broader audience.

24. The Challenges

Many of the challenges that C-level executives face are not ones that can be resolved using technical expertise or a college education. Functioning at the C-level is a totally different experience, where psychological, social, and political factors all come into play.

The complexity of information that C-level executives must process means that it is easy to become overwhelmed even with supporting staff. Without systems to manage incoming noise and data, effective decision making becomes untenable. Nancy could no longer enjoy her morning commute listening to music or a podcast. She now had to field three or four phone calls via multiple blue tooth lines on the way to work. Triaging incoming information immediately became a high priority. Nancy experienced anxiety. But anxiety can be motivating, and Nancy utilized technology to help manage the onslaught of daily communications.

Managing the Information Tidal Wave

Nancy assigned certain ringtones to high priority callers so that she knew when to pick up her phone. She automatically tagged emails that required urgent attention so that she did not skip them, and she reacted quickly to priority messages. Lastly, Nancy delegated.

25. Ambiguity

Information that is unclear or ambiguous will exist regardless. However, as a C-level executive, it was critical that Nancy immediately triaged even with ambiguity because something that is seemingly innocuous could be project threatening. Nancy had to explore the implications of any development and quickly settle on a course of action. In other words, at the C-level, ambiguity is unacceptable.

Nancy's view of the chess board at her professional level was different. She could see all the moves for every piece, and Nancy used her knowledge and perspective to choose the best strategy. Nancy used her talent to clear any ambiguity for herself, the organization, stakeholders, and her reports.

In the past, Nancy's work had been directed by her manager; however, at the C-level, Nancy became the leader. She guided her team like the North star. Nancy experienced a huge shift in mindset. She had to be one step ahead and translate the unknown business conditions to something actionable, and she could not pass any ambiguity down through the organization.

Nancy perfected the art of providing clarity every day. If she gave unclear directions, the next level would be misaligned, and the team would lose focus and direction. Under these circumstances, projects would have to be unwound.

As a leader, Nancy had experts in place to resolve ambiguity. This is the only way she could guide her team with a clear view and maintain alignment with the corporate goals. In contrast, a less mature manager, like Max, would require guidance and clear go-to-market direction from his C-level management.

26. Politics

There are always diverse interests to consider at the mid-management level. However, at the C-level, Nancy encountered many personalities from cross-functional business areas that were outside her area of expertise— sales, marketing, engineering, and global, country, and regional business heads. These personalities brought vast experience and knowledge to the table that Nancy did not have. Thus, she required leadership and deft people skills to gain the support of these inclusive cross-functional representatives.

Nancy found that being a professional at the C-level is complex. In her daily work, she interacted with people from many cultures and backgrounds; however, they were similar in one respect. Many executives were ambitious and driven. Her peers were talented, competitive individuals who had risen to the higher echelons using their wits and tenacity. She spent most of her time flexing her influence muscles.

27. Delegating

It was critical that first, second, and third-level managers deliver to Nancy the information that she needed expeditiously. Nancy supervised other managers, who possessed unique talents and core competencies. As a leader, she built the best channels of communication so that her team could communicate the real truths to her and not just what they thought she wanted to hear.

Nancy trusted her team to do their job because she spent time looking at the bigger picture. She identified the best and most trusted staff to take care of details on her behalf. One of the key things that Nancy did was to bolster her team with talent.

The decision to leave Microsoft for a startup was not an easy one for Daniel. The tech giant provided top-notch health care, competitive pay, and comprehensive benefits. But for Daniel, it was not the perfect workplace. There were many scheduling meetings, and the process of getting things done was a combination of effort and political maneuvering. Daniel decided to join a smaller company so that he could find his own path and one that would be more appealing. Now that he was over thirty years old, married but without children, he was extremely ready to build a successful career of his own.

Daniel connected to Nancy through LinkedIn. During his inter-view for chief financial officer, Nancy forced him to think hard about what he really wanted. Did he want to expand and build his own new department? Did he want the opportunity to take on other roles like corporate strategy. These avenues would be closed to him if he were with a large company. He knew then the direction he wanted to take.

The risk at that time was pre–seed investment, and although that seed funding was coming, the timing was not guaranteed. However, Daniel considered both the startup idea and the product suited to the growing market, and he took a leap of faith.

Daniel left Microsoft to become a promising director of finance at the start up under Nancy. He would not be his own boss, but he would have the freedom to succeed and fail based on his decisions. Additionally, if the jump turned out to be successful, it was due to his cultivating efforts. If it failed, he would learn some valuable lessons. Daniel had a YOLO (You Only Live Once) experience at the perfect time in his life.

For Nancy, getting Daniel on board was a great win. Daniel was both hungry and he had hands-on experience with how a finance team functioned within a giant company. Daniel became Nancy's strong go-to person for business strategy.

28. Learning

Nancy had transformed from a senior manager and developed a C-level mindset[1]. She could see the whole chess board and look at the organization holistically, inside and out. Externally, Nancy handled media communication, made sure she understood what mattered to the customers most, and kept stakeholders informed and at bay. Internally, she provided direction and managed and motivated employees. Nancy became a role model.

Becoming the Main Character

At the C-level, Nancy was no longer in a supporting role but the starring role. She was in the spotlight all the time. Nancy knew what to stop doing so that she could devote her energy to leading.

Initially, Nancy made the mistake of overmanaging research and development because that composed the vertical part of her T, and she could remain in her comfort zone. However, she learned that she had to let go if other management concerns were to receive sufficient attention.

When Nancy took on a global role, she immediately let go of the day-to-day management of engineering and became a company leader. She learned to place her research and development experience on the backburner.

---

1 The First 90 Days: Proven Strategies for Getting Up to Speed Faster and Smarter by Michael D. Watkins

Lastly, as the main character, Nancy learned that with visibility comes responsibility. Nancy was the center of attention. She was the topic of discussion at the employee lunch table, the water fountain, and in the homes of her reports. Her employees' children knew her by name. Because of her influence, Nancy made sure that her words were always carefully parsed. She encouraged team members to quote her in different contexts, and she took advantage of social media to promote the company. She learned the art of public relations (PR) and how to convey the right message.

Becoming the Spokesperson

Nancy's word carried more weight at the C-level, and more people were listening to her—customers, the media, and stakeholders. She made sure her messages were clear and devoid of ambiguity so that they could not be misinterpreted. Employees could easily quote Nancy out of context, so all conversations and presentations were carefully planned. For this reason, many companies provide media training to help executives manage PR and PR events.

Becoming a Goal Setter

Nancy was a problem solver, but her focus was giving direction and setting goals. Nancy was not on the ground identifying chemical compounds, she was at the ten-thousand-foot level giving direction and moving the team on to the next project. She did not get mired in the details. Nancy delegated, allocated resources, and trusted her team to do its job.

Becoming a Project Curator

Controlling multiple projects calls for milestones, KPIs, and delivery matrices. Nancy swam around at the water level to check whether projects were progressing, and cross-team functions were taken care of. If there was more than one situation to manage, a startup, cash cow, or adaptation, there were decisions on trade-offs, priorities, and budgets.

Either starting, canceling, or pivoting a project's direction requires organization. Nancy looked down from her elevated viewpoint and could see where bubbles were being stirred up. She looked at the cross-team functions through a strategic lens. While doing so, she directed her team like the North star while maintaining alignment.

Becoming a Visionary

As the leader, Nancy maintained a cleared mind and envisioned the future organization. This required leaving the details to others, seeing things from an elevated position, and taking a future-oriented approach. Nancy knew the details of the technical field, but she had to perfect her horizontal T and her handling of her up, down, and across relationships. As a visionary, she needed to convey her vision to others. This required nurturing relationships with her peers, board members, the public, and external networks—her whole ecosystem. Nancy needed to build partnerships with different players to realize her vision.

The Birds-eye View

Nancy dropped her vertical T activities (research and development) to attain a birds-eye view of all activities. She was now in charge of creating the structure, not the intricate interior features. Nancy strategized to avoid future avoidable setbacks. At the senior level, Nancy focused on the production line and the overall structure instead of the details or how things were being done.

Summary

When Nancy moved to the executive level, she had to let go of some responsibilities. By letting things go, she could concentrate on achieving the company vision and curating the direction of her organization. At the same time, she acquired new soft skills and used them to manage communication. The relationships changed as she became the main character.

Nancy took on volunteer services in China because she recognized her duty as a leader to empower others. In her voluntary role, she mentored and supported new managers

At the executive level, Nancy functioned like an air traffic controller. Her staff managed operations like a fleet of aircraft. Some were drones doing one task, others were helicopters that hovered and dove up, down, and around, and there were managers who acted like airline jets cruising at 30,000 feet.

As the air traffic controller, Nancy had the highest view of all. She was interacting with advisors and the board of directors. She had to manage her fleet and deliver to the board on time. Nancy had to let go of many of her tasks and allow her fleet to do their job. Once she mastered her role as air traffic controller, she became the best candidate for CEO.

PART VI.

PERSONAL GROWTH

The five stories presented in this guide narrate the personal growth that professionals may experience at various stages in their careers. The stories do not show steady progression because growth is not linear. Just as Michelle had to take a step back to learn a new industry, there are times when sacrifices are necessary in order to move forward. However, growth is a process of lifelong learning, and it always changes your perspective, your approach, and your personality.

Michelle was a first-generation Chinese American who came to the United States as a student. She began her career hoping to live the American dream and found herself in an unfamiliar cultural environment. Michelle overcame huge language and cultural barriers as she entered the American workforce.

Max was a manager and more settled in U.S. culture. He learned to manage all the relationships up, down, and around him. He built strong relationships with his direct manager, his diagonal managers, his peers, and his external network to thrive in western culture.

Kevin advanced his career to a senior general manager position by moving to China and taking on a leadership position spearheaded a startup division within a large company in his native country. He learned to operate in a new environment without his supporting network. Kevin felt that his career was stalling in the United States, and he made a huge decision to relocate the whole family back to China. In doing so, he had the additional responsibility of supporting his family through a significant life change. Kevin became an iconic leader of a Chinese entity and succeeded in arbitrating between the Chinese and American cultures, protecting his company's reputation.

Nancy broke through the glass ceiling and reached the executive level by being curious, promoting herself, and prioritizing tasks as her management responsibilities increased. She rose through the ranks of her corporation, she became a visionary, influencer, and competent project curator. She maintained her authenticity while conforming to U.S. culture. She is a role model for many career women.

You may find yourself in a similar situation to Michelle, Max, Kevin, or Nancy, or in a combination of their situations. To conclude this guide, I'd like to provide some golden nuggets and insights into personal growth and to help you open the doors to your career advancement. Whether you are in a similar position to Michelle, Max, Kevin, or Nancy, the following concepts will always apply.

29. Manifesting Personal Growth

Since the pandemic, more and more work are done remotely, which means interacting with your boss and colleagues via computer collaborative tools, like Zoom. We present ourselves at work in a small window. Therefore, verbal communication is a major part of making an impression across the digital working style.

Do you feel that you are overachieving yet undervalued? If so, there are ways to overcome this and ensure that your value is recognized. For example, Chinese Americans tend to avoid praising each other. Culturally, bragging creates tremendous guilt. Chinese Americans are taught to be humble and to think in terms of "we" instead of "I." The English language is not a strong point, and Chinese Americans hesitate to speak up because it is considered a waste of time—hard work should speak for itself.

The dilemma with this cultural behavior is that you are not visible, especially working remotely through computer media. Hard work may be appreciated, but it may not necessarily be rewarded. It is incumbent upon you to communicate what you do and what you need. You have to manifest yourself by adapting to the situation.

There are three elements to manifest yourself and your work: being proud, being bold, and planning. Being proud is recognizing your achievements, being bold is being willing to talk about your achievements, and planning is taking a measured approach to any scenario. For example, first build an online presence that is consistent and repetitive. Remote work gives you the opportunity to build a digital presence through collaboration tools like Slack, email, con-ferencing tools, blogs, and chat rooms. Plan how to take responsibil-ity for the relationships around you.

The following are practical tools that you can use to help your communication when building these relationships manifesting for your personal growth.

30. The Elevator Pitch

A well-crafted elevator pitch is a critical first step in any relationship. Your elevator pitch is a short statement that sells you as a brand. It is an essential tool that you can use in your day-to-day activities; for example, when you need to introduce yourself during a presentation, when you first meet an interviewer, or when you greet a customer. You can also use the elevator pitch as a headline for your LinkedIn page. There are many ways to prepare an elevator pitch.

Here is an example of a one-sentence elevator pitch for Michelle.

"I'm Michelle Wong. I am a software engineer who helps software companies create cloud features on AWS's end-to-end journey so the company can deliver high quality products and boost their revenues."

You can tailor the pitch depending on your situation. Here's how to construct your own.

I'm [*your name*].

I'm a [*your title—software engineer, business analyst, insurance broker, VP of operations, CEO*]

who helps [*industry or company—IT, fintech, biotech, CROs, e-commerce, education institutions, small business*]

to [*explain what you do; for example, optimize IT systems*]

so the company can [*explain what your impact is—increase revenue; reduce cost; boost their competitive edge*]."

Below are elevator pitches for Max, Kevin, and Nancy:

*"**I'm** Max. **I'm a** senior IT sales manager **who helps** my company **to** market their product lines. I work on generating leads and closing deals, **so they can** grow the revenue by 150% this year."*

*"**I'm** Kevin. **I'm** general manager of an e-commerce international division. I **help** my company **to** grow its Asian operations **so they can** expand into global markets."*

*"**I'm** Nancy. **I'm** Chief Medical Officer **who helps** biotech companies **to** stay on the front line of drug discovery **so they can** deliver their unique value proposition to customers and achieve competitive advantage.*

Nancy used this one-sentence statement during a presentation to the key board members. Her presentation, which began with her elevator pitch, impressed the board so much that they chose her as the next CEO. Her statement presented her as a confident leader, she was concise, direct, and on top of her game.

Some first-generation immigrant American managers may state what they do well, but they sometimes fail to consider who they are talking to. Helping the listener to understand their role whether the listener is the CEO or someone from another industry is critical as a leader. In addition to a great elevator pitch, it's wise to prepare elevator pitches for parties, gatherings and other social occasions.

31. Getting to the Point (PREP: Point-Reason-Example-Point Again)

PREP is a tool that stands for Point-Reason-Example-Point Again (PREP). The PREP tool is a way to communicate your ideas to your audience clearly, concisely, and persuasively. Your audience wants you to get to the point fast.

If you want to present a point, to give the background first before delivering the headline is not culturally fit. American culture favors the opposite approach—giving the headline first and then the explanation, which is a 180-degree pivot.

Here's how to communicate using PREP:

Point: Identify the point you are trying to make.

Reason: Give the reasoning behind the point you are delivering.

Example: Give an example of your suggestion with back-up data.

Point Again: Reiterate your original point to reinforce the message.

Max felt that he had been given an opportunity as a manager, and he wanted to take full advantage of it. He applied PREP to make sure his messages were clear and to maximize the likelihood that his audience would agree with him. PREP helped him to build influence. Here is how Max presented a proposal for the launch date for his new product:

> *"I think we should push the launch date out two weeks [Point] because we don't want our launch to be lost*

with the holiday noise and lose impact [Reason]. Our last product launch was right before the holidays, and most of our customers were busy preparing for family events. That meant we lost significant media coverage for 48 hours, which damaged sales [Example]. It's crucial that we learn from that experience and push the launch out another two weeks. [Point again].

In meetings, Max was often interrupted while he was presenting his point, but he was able to carry on with his message when he had the opportunity without losing his train of thought. He returned to the PREP tool and continued. Learning to present issues this way will train your thinking process and help you develop, clear, concise, and more powerful communication habits.

32. The Communication Eye

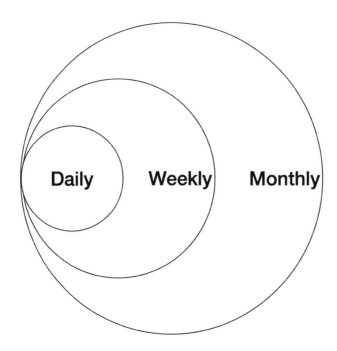

Figure 4 Personal Communication Network

The communication eye is a tool that maps your communication network. With the communication eye map, you can plan who you must communicate with on a daily, weekly, and monthly basis. This is important if you are to maintain relationships that will help your career.

The inner circle shows who you should interact with daily. For example, daily scrums, face-to-face meetings, emails, phone calls, chats, or Slack posts.

The next circle shows who you should check in with on a weekly basis. These could be weekly one-on-ones with individual contributors from your team, project managers, or product owners who directly impact your work. In the outer part of the eye are the individuals that you should communicate with on a monthly basis. They could be peers in the next department or in regional offices.

There will be some people who you rarely communicate with— customers or indirect peers. But it is important that you maintain a connection with these people too. It is particularly critical that you leave a good impression with these connections because the memory that the person has of you will last until the two of you meet again, which could be a long time.

The eye shows you who you need to check in with and when. Your eye will change as your work progresses. Some of your weekly conversations may become your daily conversations depending on the critical mass of your projects.

Kevin had multi-network global relationships to manage. He used the eye to keep his networking on track. He developed a clear view of his position and maintained relationships with key people throughout the corporation. He used the eye to gain the influence and support he needed to enter new markets and double his company's top-line revenue growth.

33. The S Curve. A Technique for Answering Questions

The S curve, or bridging, is a way to transition from a question to a message. Mirroring the curves of the letter S, first, acknowledge the question or idea. Second, use transition words, phrases or a sentence; Third, continue to curve and bridge into what you want to say—flash out your real messages. Bridging is useful when in meetings or answering an interview or media questions. It is particularly useful when addressing unfamiliar issues. You will find several examples of bridging in the following scenarios.

Nancy was having to respond to a lot of media questions as an executive. Too often, she allowed the reporters to lead the press events. She wanted to leave a positive public image and create a favorable impression, so she would simply answer one question after another. The problem was that she rarely had the opportunity to deliver the right message.

Nancy used a bridging technique to allow her to pivot from a reporter's question and to deliver her intended message following the S curve.

S curve bridging is a critical technique that helped Nancy respond to off-topic, difficult, or hostile questions. She did not want to respond to skeptical questioning during an interview because she might come across as being defensive. She wanted to deliver the right message and not miss the opportunity to influence her investors.

Politicians often use the bridging technique to transition to what they want to say. Here are some examples of S curve bridge phrases:

"What matters the most to our customers is…."

"The most important thing to remember is…"

"That's not what we have been experiencing from our customers. What we've been hearing from the customer is…"

"That said, what we saw as an even bigger problem is…"

S curve bridging can be interpreted as intentionally skipping the question, but it is really a way to avoid answering the question directly so that their audience will not disagree with their views.

Bridging in a job interview could be a problem if used more than one or two times in 30 minutes of conversation or inappropriately. It could appear that the interviewee does not understand the subject. Used smoothly, the technique can yield great results.

The transition should be short, a phrase or a single word. For example:

- Sure
- Well
- Yes
- No
- Maybe
- Perhaps
- Right
- That's not what our data says
- I am not sure about that
- Partially, the complete answer is…

These phrases can precede the transition to the S curve bridge and to your message.

Here's an Example. *Kevin represents an environmental non-profit working to protect the American gray wolf in Montana. Many residents are upset with a proposal for a conservation area because they fear Kevin's group is prioritizing the wolf over the concerns of nearby residents.*

The message Kevin wants to get across is this:

"Protecting the American gray wolf will boost ecotourism, the local economy, and the quality of life for local residents and their families."

Here's the reporter's question:

"Isn't there inevitably going to be conflict whenever environmentalists propose a new conservation area that impacts local residents?"

The danger here is that Kevin's response will address the conflict between environmentalists and residents, rather than convey Kevin's message, which is how the proposal will improve the local economy. Using a bridge allows Kevin to answer the question, but then to pivot and deliver his message.

[Answer] "There is no conflict. [Bridge] What I hope nearby residents will keep in mind is that [Message] protecting the American gray wolf can help people in the area earn a better living because the increase in ecotourism will significantly boost local business. We know this because three years ago, residents in Montana were nervous about a new conservation area—but we now know that the people living next to that area saw an increase in their household income."

One final note: Save your bridges for moments that matter. If you use too many of them in a single interview, the message could be perceived as disingenuous.

34. Integrating Personal, Relational, and Positional Power

A huge component of professional advancement is the ability to influence. Each of us has our own skills and attributes that we can leverage in our relationships. The three main powers to be aware of are personal, relational, and positional power. These three powers need to be carefully balanced.

Personal Power: Your personal power is your T-shape. The vertical part of the T is your technical skills, and the horizontal part of the T is your functional capabilities, or your cross-department skills; for example, how knowledgeable you are in non-technical areas like marketing or finance. You should aim to grow and balance the vertical and horizontal parts of your T so that you not only understand the technology of a product, but you can also discuss the marketing and financial aspects of it at a sufficient level.

Relational Power: Relational power is how you leverage your technical skills and establish your expertise. This is a valuable soft skill to perfect, and much of it is dependent on your management of communication and networks.

Positional power: Positional power is how much influence you have through your work. Positional power is not related to your hierarchical level but the value the company places in what you do. For example, the project manager of a flagship product at a fintech possesses a lot more power than the VP of operations because of the significance of the flagship product in the company's product portfolio.

If these three powers are balanced correctly, you can use them to influence your manager, your diagonal managers, and your peers. An example of influence is that as you interact with various people, you will undoubtedly do certain things for them, and they will do things for you in return. Therefore, your influence yields power.

When your powers are balanced, the result is like a fountain where the water is forced up, comes down, and is constantly circulating. This fountain represents the relationships that should be effortless with your boss, your peers, your customers, and your team. Creating this balance and flow is a fine art, and it is incredibly powerful if mastered.

35. Deep Inner Growth (DEG: Distraction-Empowering-Growth)

As you progress along your career journey to a new height, there are a lot of relationships that need to be reestablished even though your boss, peers and team members worked with you before. This is a good time to reflect on your mental strength as you take on increasing responsibility. Your previous boss is now your peer on the organization chart. How can you position yourself at a new level to break the glass ceiling without breaking your good working relationship? How can you find ways to work with the person who has applied for the same position and did not get the promotion? How can you calibrate the new team dynamic to manage up, manage down and manage around new peers? You will need to find ways to tackle priorities, process emotions, and understand the psychological changes that occur as you mature professionally.

The visibility of senior leadership means that they face constant criticism—it comes with the CEO and senior leadership territory—and criticism can be difficult to manage without a strong support network that includes advisors, mentors, family, and friends. DEG (**D**istraction-**E**mpowering-**G**rowth) is a tool you can use to manage the inner turmoil that you might experience in your career growth journey.

Distraction:

The emails, Slack messages, and social messaging that you are bombarded with are other people's priorities and not necessarily yours. Triaging all this information and prioritizing your time helps to calm the noise. The thought of taking on a particularly pressing task can seem overwhelming. One approach is to eliminate all other distractions for as long as you can, and just make a start.

Initially, you might be able to devote just twenty minutes to a task. Set a timer and focus for those twenty minutes. Then, plan to devote another twenty minutes when you can. The goal is to get to a point where you have something to work with. In agile methodology, this process is called "collaborative problem framing." From here, you can continue to the next stage or iteration.

Empowering:

At the executive level, it is easy to take things for granted and to focus on yourself to the exclusion of others. But that's a mistake. As a leader, you should stay engaged, listen, stay hungry and curious, and maintain your authenticity by mentoring and empowering others. Become a servant leader.

Growth mindset:

When you are an executive, how you react to feedback will dictate how the public views your decision-making thought process. An advisor or a career coach to give you a more objective perspective. As you grow, others will increasingly give you, their opinions. You are constantly looking for ways to use your valuable time to be creative, curious, and assertive. By triaging incoming noise in today's explosive information age, removing distractions when you need to focus on priorities, managing your mental and physical strength, and being aware of your calling to empower others, you stay hungry and sustain a growth mindset.

DEG is a tool that you can apply to all levels of corporate management and your personal life. When Kevin moved up to a senior leadership position, he encountered an aspect of professional maturity that is often overlooked. He could no longer maintain the same relationships he once had. DEG helped him to recognize this symptom of growth and helped him to manage his experience with the help from advisors, mentors, family and friends.

Kevin said to his report once as he was mentoring his next level manager: Sometimes being the person on top is never easy. Because you are the North Star for the whole organization, if you make decisions based on what is the best for the customers that the company serves, your decision should always be solid and serve the business's longevity well.

36. The Power of Great Questions

How important is it to ask great questions? What and how we ask our questions is of greater value than the answers. Chinese people are trained to perfect their answers from the first day of school. The better your answer the more successful you will be. As we develop in our American careers, however, asking the right questions impacts our relationships with the people around us. The quality of our questions is extremely valuable. Silicon Valley is created by curiosity that starts with a great question. There are some techniques to funnel these questions at the right time. Any question is a good one—there are no bad questions—what matters most is asking the right questions at the right time. The impact of a leader who asks the wrong questions can lead to massive derailment and loss of focus for the organization.

There are two types of questions, open-ended and closed. Open-ended questions are usually phrased using "how" and "why," closed questions are answered with "yes" or "no."

For conversations, open-ended questions are better than closed questions because they require a longer answer and stimulate ideas. You can become more valuable at work just by asking the right questions. Here are a few examples of open-ended questions that will give you power in meetings and discussions:

> *1. Situation: What is happening? What is happening at the moment?*

2. Clarification: Tell me why? Why do you say that?

3. Probe: Can we assume this is the case? Is there another possibility?

4. Viewpoint: What is your perspective? Is there another way to look at this?

5. Reasons and evidence: What would be a good example of this? When did that occur?

6. Consequences: How does not doing this impact the situation? What would happen if we did not do this?

These questions will help to clarify a situation.

37. The STAR Method

Figure 5 STAR Method[2]

When some immigrant Americans spontaneously communicate or debate business or technical issues, English communication skills raise the level of competition. There are so many things to think about when communicating in a non-native language—the logic, the vocabulary, the culture, the business domain, technical acumen. Complex communication can flow very well using the STAR framework to outline the idea following a pre-designed structure.

The STAR model is used by many professionals in different scenarios. The model can help anyone to steer a path in meetings, job interviews, presentations, Q&A sessions, and negotiations. Let's break down the STAR framework. STAR is an acronym that stands for the following:

---

2 DDI invented the STAR method as one of the simplest and most effective ways to communicate in an interview or when providing feedback. The STAR method is a powerful tool for every leader.

Situation: Set the scene and give the necessary details of the example.

Task: Describe the tasks or work for that situation.

Action: Explain exactly what steps you took to execute the task.

Result: Conclude the outcomes of the actions.

Using these four components to shape the story simplifies the delivery of a focused answer and provides the listener with a digestible but compelling story.

Answering Interview Questions Using STAR

Knowing what the acronym stands for is the first step. Once you understand the concept, practice your delivery, and use it in all communication where applicable.

———————

Michelle used the STAR framework when she interviewed for her senior software developer positions after her successful elevator pitch. The STAR interview method wouldn't be helpful for Michelle if she used it to structure an answer using a totally irrelevant story. That's why the crucial starting point is to find an appropriate scenario from her professional history that she could expand upon.

Before the interview, Michelle prepared thoroughly. She did not know ahead of time exactly what the interviewer would ask her although she knew there was a list of interview questions on behavior that she could predict. She had a few stories and outlined examples ready to go, and she could adapt on the spot depending on what questions the interviewer asked.

Following the job history on her resume, she prepared an anecdote for each job and skill using the STAR framework. She repeated that exercise for various types of questions.

With her anecdote selected, she set the scene. It was tempting to include all sorts of unnecessary details—particularly when her nerves get the better of her. She knew that if the interview asked her to recall a time, she didn't meet a client's expectations, for example, they did not need to know how she recruited the client three years earlier or the entire history of the project.

Her goal was to paint a clear picture of the situation and emphasize its complexities, so that the result she touched on later seemed that much more profound. She kept things concise and focused on what was undeniably relevant to her story. If she provided too much detail, her answers would be too long. She decided to focus on just one or two sentences for each letter of the STAR acronym.

Here is a step-by-step process for clear and to-the-point STAR communication using Michelle's interview as an example.

Situation

The interviewer asked Michelle, *"Tell me about a time when you accomplished a task that you thought was impossible to achieve."*

Michelle: *"In my last software engineering role, my company made the decision to focus primarily on Cloud and was looking to increase new user subscribers pretty aggressively."*

Task

Michelle had some core involvement in the project. This part of her answer is where she described exactly where she fit in the new job.

Michelle: *"As the senior software developer, my target was to increase my knowledge in the Cloud area and build functions to increase new customers by 50% in just one quarter."*

Action

Michelle had given the interviewer a sense of her role. She explained what she did and what steps she took to reach that goal or solve that problem. Michelle needed to grab the listener's attention by elaborating on the details of the task she did in steps. Not just saying, "I worked hard." This was Michelle's chance to really show-case her contribution, and it is worthy of some specifics. Michelle should provide details on exactly what she did—the team name, the specifics of the software. These are the things the interviewer wants to know.

Michelle: *"I started by going back through old performance issues and created information for the knowledge base. This immediately gave our customer a confidence boost by 50% according to the survey. Next, I worked with the rest of the community team to plan and host a webinar. That brought 5 times more interested users to our download page for our free trial."*

Result

Michelle manifested her cross-functional influence from marketing to engineering. She went the extra mile to make a difference. The final portion of her response were the results of the action she took. The results were positive.

Michelle delivered a success story. If the outcome had not been a success, and she had made a mistake, she could have focused on the learning and ended on a high note by talking about the steps she took to improve her approach.

———

Michelle delivered her story and closed the STAR framework with a question: *"This is how I handled the situation, but it might not be the only way. I would be interested if you have any feedback on my approach?*

The interviewers want to know what Michelle did, and why it mattered. It may not be in words directly, solidifying any results and quantifying them in numbers is very powerful.

Michelle: *"As a result of those additions to our solution, the company was able to increase our new trial list to 40,000 subscribers in three months. That exceeded our goal by 20%."*

As another example. Here's one more question from the manager:

"How would you ensure that we are strategic in meeting all of our top priorities in the coming quarter?"

Answer: *"In our last project, I was put in charge of the transfer to an entirely new customer relationship management (CRM) system on top of handling my daily sales calls and responsibilities. (**Situation**). The goal was to have the migration to the new CRM database completed* *by Q3, without letting any of our sales numbers slip below the targets.* *(**T**ask)*

In order to do that, we were very careful about how we managed all our project timelines. I dedicated an hour each day solely to the CRM migration for the team. During that time, we collaborated on transferring the data as well as cleaning out old contacts and updating outdated information. This gave the team enough time to process the details while still handling our normal tasks. *(**A**ction)*

As a result, the transfer was completed two weeks ahead of the deadline, and we finished the quarter ten percent over our team sales goal." *(**R**esult)*

The STAR model for answering questions might seem a little rigid at first, but with practice it will become a habit. For some meetings, you can practice the answers with family or a Zoom recording. Talking through the answers will help you to feel natural and comfortable when you are in a real meeting. With just a little practice and planning, you'll soon view spontaneous questions as less of a pressure and more of an awesome meeting experience.

These tools, as golden nuggets, will mold you into a much better leader as you emerge from what can be a difficult period.

———————

In closing, immigrants working in corporate America fulfill the diversity complement of the corporate landscape. As trailblazing pioneers, by gaining a better understanding of ourselves and the American corporate culture, we can change the approaches in a way that improves both global business and our own careers. We are all on our journey to our next advancement, and it is a lifetime journey. By taking the best of melting pot attributes, first-generation immigrant business leaders in American companies pioneered the path for many generations to come. New immigrants from all over the world continue this trend to work without borders. We have seen immigrants make a great impact in many industries and fields. We are unique pathfinders in our own way to help the world to be a better place.

PATHFINDER: A GUIDE TO A SUCCESSFUL CAREER FOR FIRST-GENERATION IMMIGRANTS

Most first-generation immigrants harbor lofty ambitions when they begin their journey to America. Many of these individuals have aced rigorous exams, their outstanding performance has placed them at the top of their class in universities, and their college years have earned them high honors from their classmates, professors, and families. Without a doubt, expectations are high for these proud individuals. As young trailblazers, they feel pressure to succeed and prove that the sacrifice of their parents and past generations has not been in vain. As the cream of the crop, professional achievement is not just expected for these young people, it is considered a duty. But ambiguity and obstacles await them as they embark on their professional journey in America.

What are the challenges for these young, ambitious, first-generation immigrant pioneers, and how can they overcome the barriers of learning, language, and culture? How can they compete in a fierce work environment, earn recognition, and advance to senior management in corporate America?

Among these first-generation immigrants are Chinese students who began to arrive in the United States after 1972 when China opened the door to study in America. In the 1980s, more Chinese scholars journeyed to America and other overseas countries for academic and scientific research work. For America, Chinese students were a new business and academic market, and in the1990s the country saw an influx of Chinese students with increasing influence.

They were trailblazers. They were brave, intelligent, and curious, and their experiences represent fascinating case studies for later generations. Today's Asian-Americans who are entering and navigating western business can learn and build upon the experiences of those who came before them.

This book uses the stories of five first-generation immigrant pioneers to show the challenges faced by new immigrants eager to succeed in American business. They show managers moving up to manage managers and learning to deal with senior management challenges. The stories honestly reveal the norms, communication styles, mindsets, and politics of corporate business to help other brave souls newly embarking on the same path. These are not things taught in business schools; they are the life experiences of a generation.

Most first-generation immigrants harbor lofty ambitions when they begin their journey to America. Many of these individuals have aced rigorous exams, their outstanding performance has placed them at the top of their class in universities, and their college years have earned them high honors from their classmates, professors, and families. Without a doubt, expectations are high for these proud individuals. As young trailblazers, they feel pressure to succeed and prove that the sacrifice of their parents and past generations has not been in vain. As the cream of the crop, professional achievement is not just expected for these young people, it is considered a duty. But ambiguity and obstacles await them as they embark on their professional journey in America.

What are the challenges for these young, ambitious, first-generation immigrant pioneers, and how can they overcome the barriers of learning, language, and culture? How can they compete in a fierce work environment, earn recognition, and advance to senior management in corporate America?

Among these first-generation immigrants are Chinese students who began to arrive in the United States after 1972 when China opened the door to study in America. In the 1980s, more Chinese scholars journeyed to America and other overseas countries for academic and scientific research work. For America, Chinese students were a new business and academic market, and in the1990s the country saw an influx of Chinese students with increasing influence.

They were trailblazers. They were brave, intelligent, and curious, and their experiences represent fascinating case studies for later generations. Today's Asian-Americans who are entering and navigating western business can learn and build upon the experiences of those who came before them.

This book uses the stories of five first-generation immigrant pioneers to show the challenges faced by new immigrants eager to succeed in American business. They show managers moving up to manage managers and learning to deal with senior management challenges. The stories honestly reveal the norms, communication styles, mindsets, and politics of corporate business to help other brave souls newly embarking on the same path. These are not things taught in business schools; they are the life experiences of a generation.